GOD IS WITH US:

Daily Reflections for Advent

John J. McIlhon

THE LITURGICAL PRESS
Collegeville, Minnesota 56321

Cover by Joshua Jeide, O.S.B.

Nihil obstat: Frank E. Bognanno, J.C.D., *Censor deputatus.*

Imprimatur: ✝ William H. Bullock, D.D., Bishop of Des Moines, July 5, 1989.

3	4	5	6	7	8	9	10

Library of Congress Cataloging-in-Publication Data

McIlhon, John.
   God is with us : daily reflections for Advent / John J. McIlhon ; foreword by James Jones.
      p. cm.
   ISBN 0-8146-1898-7
      1. Advent—Meditations. 2. Catholic Church. Liturgy of the Hours (U.S., et al.)—Meditations. I. Title.
BX2170.A4M4   1989   89-13138
242' .33—dc20   CIP

Contents

Preface

I would be less than honest if I said that Advent has always had deep meaning for me. The truth of the matter is, it had little meaning until one of St. Bernard's homilies opened a meaning of Advent that had not been a major concern of my school days' catechesis.

I had been well taught that "Advent" means "coming." I had been instructed that this first season of the Church's liturgical year celebrated the comings of Christ both in Bethlehem and at the end of time. But quite frankly, I could not reason the taking of four weeks' valuable worshiping time to celebrate comings whose remote meanings hardly touched my life, other than, it seemed, to wind me up for Christmas and for the end of the world.

When the newly revised *Liturgy of the Hours* replaced the daily breviary, I little suspected that the "Sermon by St. Bernard, abbot," in the Office of Readings for Wednesday of Advent's first week would become a major Advent blessing for me. "We know," he writes, "that there are three comings of the Lord. The third lies between the other two" (see "Reflection," p. 18). From that moment, insights about this beautiful season, upon which this book reflects, began to unfold. From these insights it became apparent to me that Advent is not confined to a past coming of Christ nor to his future coming in glory. Advent is also about a coming *now!*

This book is not meant to undermine the past and future comings of Christ. Its purpose is to call readers' attention to the coming of Christ that "lies between the other two." There is nothing we can do about the "other two," but the "third coming" of Christ can make a tremendous difference in our lives. This is the coming that will enable the season of Advent to bring to Christ's coming a meaning that will "prepare the way of the Lord" (Isa 40:3) into our lives, now!

Like my previous effort, *Forty Days Plus Three: Daily Reflections for Lent and Holy Week* (The Liturgical Press), this book has been designed to help readers prayerfully examine the coming that Christ seeks to offer us every day. Based on the Office of Readings from the Church's *Liturgy of the Hours,* each chapter of this book comprises three parts, "Word," "Reflection," and "Questions for Your Reflection." A few moments each day with this format will be a well-coming for that "coming" of Advent you may little suspect.

The Church's Advent treasury contains much more for our spiritual enrichment than preparations for Christmas and the glorious coming of Christ yet to come. Advent pleads with us to embrace a coming of Christ seeking entry into our lives *every* day of the year. This is the coming that enables us to be at peace even when little peace is in our midst. "And know that I am with you always, until the end of the world!" (Matt 28:20) May I offer this hope—this certainty—for readers who begin this daily Advent pilgrimage.

John J. McIlhon

Foreword

Advent has always been my favorite season. The old Gregorian chants *(Ad te levavi animam meam; Rorate coeli desuper)*, the "O" antiphons at Vespers toward the end of Advent, the haunting feeling of expectation, meant—and mean—a great deal to me.

Forty-five years ago, when Monsignor McIlhon and I were fellow students in the seminary, part of our German class work was reading Fr. Pius Parsch's *Das Jahr des Heiles.* It was easy German and Father Parsch spoke of three comings of Jesus: In history, in mystery, and in majesty. It's about his coming in mystery that the author is concerned in this work.

Although I am taken by everything in these pages, the Questions for Your Reflection each day are especially helpful. They bring the glories of Advent and of Christ's coming to my level. The answers to those questions are often very frightening and demanding—as is the entire Gospel of the Lord.

Early on our author asks: "If God does not seem near to you, who moved?" It is a provocative question.

The Fathers of Vatican II dreamt of the day when liturgists would be more concerned with theology—pastoral theology. Monsignor McIlhon's book, by making use of the Old Testament, the New Testament, the Fathers of the Church, and his personal experience, has made an excellent attempt to do just that.

I feel certain that serious readers of *God Is With Us* will be aided in quenching their thirst at the majestic fountain of the Advent liturgy, a fountain of living water which leads to life eternal. That fountain is Christ. *Come, Lord Jesus, Savior of your people, come and set us free, Lord our God.*

ABBOT JAMES JONES, O.S.B.
CONCEPTION ABBEY

Who Moved?

WORD

"Hear, O heavens, and listen, O earth,
for the LORD speaks:
[Children] have I raised and reared,
but they have disowned me.
An ox knows its owner,
and an ass, its master's manger;
But Israel does not know,
my people has not understood" (Isa 1:2-3).

REFLECTION

In the home of one of my friends hangs this small sign: "If God doesn't seem close to you, who moved?"

"Advent" means "coming." This wondrous season proclaims and celebrates the God who has come, who is all around us, and who will never move away from us. Advent's voice joins Isaiah's in calling God "Immanuel," which means "God is with us" (Isa 7:14). If God has come to be close to us but is perceived as a stranger, who "moved" if God seems to be far away?

It was very clear to Isaiah that God's people had disowned their Lord. How ironic, he grieved, that "an ox knows its owner, and an ass, its master's manger; but Israel does not know, [nor have the] people understood." How clear to Isaiah that God's own children had moved, not God.

Isaiah's grief ran as deep as the estrangement he perceived. He stood before a people who arrogantly believed themselves to be one with God in a relationship they thought impeccably sound. They dutifully

9

offered sacrifices and performed external rites whose meaning had long since escaped them. Isaiah voiced God's disapproval:

> What care I for the numbers of your sacrifices?
> > says the LORD.
> I have had enough of whole-burnt rams
> > and fat of fatlings;
> In the blood of calves, lambs and goats
> > I find no pleasure. . . .
> When you spread out your hands,
> > I close my eyes to you;
> Though you pray the more,
> > I will not listen (Isa 1:11, 15).

God did not condemn ritualizing. He condemned ritualizing without meaning. God's own people had moved away from ritual's significance. The people offered sacrifices designed to signify God's deep concern for human dignity—a concern they had removed from the center of their hearts. Their relationship with God was based on ritual making as the central issue of their lives, while the issues of ritual *meaning* sat precariously on the periphery of their lives. Isaiah cried out God's deepest concern:

> Make justice your aim: redress the wronged,
> > hear the orphan's plea, defend the widow (Isa 1:16).

Advent proclaims the coming of Christ and his kingdom. When we proclaim Advent liturgically we ritualize on Christ's terms. Christ's presence in our lives is not a certainty simply because we scrupulously observe innumerable external signs. God's word to the Israelites is for us too. Enough of the rituals if there is not at the center of our lives Christ's own central issue, the issue that is the meaning of rites! Christ's central issue? It is justice, indelibly imprinted on our human dignity. All men and women were created in God's image and likeness. Ritual without dedication to this justifying meaning is superstition.

Let there be no mistake. Christ has come! Christ is Immanuel—he is with us! What *hasn't* come is the fullest meaning of Christ's coming. Christ has come that we might have at the center of our lives what is always at the center of his life—human dignity and the justice that is human dignity's infallible guarantee.

Advent challenges us to move from our lips to our hearts what hearts long to do. The will of God does not dwell on our lips, it dwells in our hearts. "None of those who cry out, 'Lord, Lord,' will enter the kingdom of God but only the one who does the will of my Father in heaven" (Matt 7:21). Those who long for the coming of human dignity among victims of injustice have at the center of their hearts the will of God. Those who have Christ at the center of their hearts have heard God's never-ending Advent message proclaimed from the heart of Isaiah: "Make justice your aim."

In 1971 the Synod of Bishops left no doubt about the place of justice in the Church's preaching and mission:

"Action on behalf of justice and participation in the transformation of the world fully appear to us as a constitutive dimension of the preaching of the Gospel, or, in other words, the Church's mission for the redemption of the human race and its liberation from every oppressive situation."[1]

Constitutive! Yes! Justice is on the Church's lips and in the Church's heart. Justice and human dignity are not on the periphery of Catholic faith. If justice is at the center of our faith, our rituals will have meaning, and God will be there. No, God has not "moved."

QUESTIONS FOR YOUR REFLECTION

1. "If God seems far away, who moved?" Why is this a good Advent question?

2. The basis of human dignity and justice is "Let us make man in our image, after our likeness" (Gen 1:26). How is this text linked to human dignity and justice?

3. What is the difference between the ways the world measures justice and the way God measures justice? Upon what does the world base human dignity? How does God measure it?

4. Justice is a "constitutive dimension" of the Church's preaching and mission. What are some other essentials of Catholic faith that constitute the Church's preaching and mission? What does the word "constitutive" mean?

Hope Is Not Wishful Thinking

WORD

"He shall judge between the nations,
and impose terms on many peoples.
They shall beat their swords into plowshares
and their spears into pruning hooks;
One nation shall not raise the sword against another,
nor shall they train for war again" (Isa 2:4).

REFLECTION

Advent invites us to revisit hope—to be aware that hope is not wishful thinking. When it dawns on us that hope is certainty, not wishfulness, our eagerness to journey into the future will generate joyful expectations we can count on.

The Church always finds herself at the point of tension where past and future meet. Because hope is certainty, the Church proclaims the good news that each tension-filled moment of the encounter of past and future is filled with the fruits of peace and joy.

The present is endangered not because a tension between past and future exists but because there lurks the temptation to embrace only one or the other. When only the past is embraced, hope's certainty becomes little more than déjà vu. When only the future is embraced, hope's certainty becomes little more than the conviction that déjà vu has nothing to offer.

God's gift of hope is certain about the future because it can point to the past's evidence of God's undaunted fidelity. The certainties of God's fidelity are also certainties valid now and for all time. There is evidence that God judges "between the nations" on the basis of certainties that shall never pass, certainties that never cease inviting us to welcome both their past and future coming.

Isaiah was crystal clear about this. He never ceased pointing to the certainty of justice, whose evidence or lack thereof formed the basis of God's judgment. Crying out to Jerusalem, he lamented:

How has she turned adulteress,
   the faithful city, so upright!
Justice used to lodge within her,
   but now murderers. . . .
The fatherless they defend not,
   and the widow's plea does not reach them (Isa 1:21-23).

From Isaiah's point of view, nothing was more certain than God's fidelity to human dignity. This was a certainty that described hope. We are called to embrace the certainty of hope despite the uncertainty of how exactly its future will be shaped. If justice is our aim, we can meet the tensions of the present moment with calm and peace. As Christians, we can embrace justice because we have the evidence of past certainty about human dignity, encouraging us to embrace the future without a moment's hesitation.

The certainty of hope that Advent proclaims is of a reality already in our midst. The tensions of hope spring from our reluctance to trust the power of Christ's redemption. St. Charles Borromeo writes: "The Church asks us to understand that Christ, who came once in the flesh, is prepared to come again. When we remove all obstacles to his presence he will come, at any hour or moment, to dwell spiritually in our hearts, bringing with him the riches of his grace."[2]

Advent celebrates a coming that is "already" but "not yet." Christ and the fully revealed certainty of justice's shape are "not yet" because sinfulness gives the illusion that they haven't come. Sin blinds us to the centrality of Christ in our lives. Christ is in our midst, but when sin reigns, we, not Christ, have moved out on the periphery of human purpose. Be that as it may "he will come, at any hour or moment. . . ." That's certain!

Speaking in God's name, Isaiah imposes "terms on many peoples" (Isa 2:4). God's terms call for the justice that liberates human dignity, a justice that restores the fundamental belonging whose sense of security inspires peace. Justice is the imperative of human purpose. Humanity belongs to God because God created all men and women to share the very life of God. That's the essence of human dignity and why justice is its imperative. It guarantees humanity's inner craving for a belonging whose fruit is freedom and peace.

What are God's terms?

[Nations] shall beat their swords into plowshares
   and their spears into pruning hooks;

One nation shall not raise the sword against another,
    nor shall they train for war again (Isa 2:4).

These are God's terms, enabling us to come joyfully to the realization that hope is much more than wishful thinking.

QUESTIONS FOR YOUR REFLECTION

1. From your experience, can you think of examples of realities which you already possessed but which had yet to come?

2. What are your thoughts on this? The only people Jesus could not reach were those whose sense of justice was rooted in a legal perspective of dignity rather than in the perspective of human dignity's purpose, God's image and likeness.

3. A bumper sticker reads: "I found it." Why is this spiritually lethal?

4. If Christmas were moved to another date, away from Advent's orbit, would Advent lose its meaning? Does Advent embrace a coming beyond Christ's historical coming?

TUESDAY OF THE FIRST WEEK

How Much Does God's Glory Weigh?

WORD

*"On that day man will throw to the moles and the bats
the idols of silver and gold which they made for worship.*

*They go into caverns in the rock
    and into crevices in the cliffs,
From the terror of the LORD
    and the splendor of his majesty,
    when he arises to overawe the earth.*

*As for you, let man alone,
    in whose nostrils is but a breath;
    for what is he worth?"* (Isa 2:20-22)

REFLECTION

The word "glory" once meant "weight." The one whose possessions weighed more than the possessions of others was regarded as the person of "glory."

It is abundantly clear from the pages of Sacred Scripture that the weight of possessions carries little weight with God. God's answer to Isaiah's question, "For what is he worth?" throughout the pages of Scripture clearly reveals a criterion this world cannot weigh.

God weighs glory not by the weight of what a person has but by the weight of who a person is. The glory of human nature is not weighed by possessions this world offers but by human nature's capacity to become the image and likeness of God.

Paradoxically, there is in the mind of God a relationship between God's glory and the spirit of poverty. If what we don't possess weighs little in the world's estimation of human worth, we weigh much in God's estimation of humanity's true worth. If what we don't possess of this world's goods weighs much with God, it is a weight easily borne. "Take my yoke upon your shoulders and learn from me, for I am gentle and humble of heart. Your souls will find rest, for my yoke is easy and my burden light" (Matt 11:29-30).

Jesus constantly faced the mentality of quantitative religion. A striking example is St. Luke's account of the rich young man (see Luke 18:18-25). This story makes clear where Christ stood with respect to religion of possessing versus religion of becoming.

A rich young man from the ruling class came to Jesus and asked, "What must I do to share in everlasting life?"

Jesus' reply was on the level of the young man's quantitative question, "What must I do . . . ?" He replied with a quantitative response:

"You shall not commit adultery.
You shall not kill.
You shall not steal.
You shall not bear dishonest witness.
Honor your father and your mother" (Luke 18:20).

Jesus' reply carried little weight with the young man because he was convinced that he already possessed the glory of keeping the commandments. Looking for more weighty religion, he answered: "I have kept all these since I was a boy."

At this point, Jesus completely disarmed him. He invited him to abandon the religious mentality of having and doing for one that longs for growth in the image and likeness of God. "There is one thing further you must do." The one thing further he must do was divest himself of *having* this world's goods ("Sell all you have and give to the poor") so that he might "have treasure in heaven."

Jesus' reply was a delicate transition from earth's having to heaven's having. To have treasure in heaven was to be fully alive in the image and likeness of God. Jesus struck at the foundation of quantitative religion, a perspective that enjoyed an erroneous authenticity among the rich and the devout of Jesus' time. The rich young man was no exception. His way, truth, and life were riches of this world, well within his capacity to have, rather than the "weight" of sharing God's glory.

The young man's riches had become his very identity. This identity carried little weight with Jesus. Jesus invited him to discard it by selling its image and likeness in behalf of the poor. The young man was devastated, for he believed ever so devoutly that the poor were anathema to God.

While we have no record of the rich young man's thoughts, we have his striking reaction to Christ's words. "Hearing these words, the young man went away sad, for his possessions were many" (Matt 19:22).

Although Jesus commented that "it is easier for a camel to go through a needle's eye than for a rich man to enter the kingdom of heaven" (Luke 18:24-25), he did not condemn this world's possessions. Jesus condemned an attitude that measures human worth by this world's possessions. The rich young man was not a bad person, nor were his possessions. What Jesus condemned was his abdication of worth measured by God's purpose for humanity. The rich young man had measured his human worth by this world's criterion of human purpose—having and doing.

The rich young man asked for an advent far removed from the advent Jesus was prepared to grant him. He asked for a coming of more things to do for God as a sign of the quantitative glory he craved. He saw no link between the glory of God's creatorship and the poverty of creaturehood that was indispensible for sharing the glory God created humanity to become. Far removed from the young man's spiritual perspective was the perspective of link between God's creatorship and humankind's creaturehood. This is the advent perspective Jesus had in mind when he invited the rich young man to "Come and follow me" (Luke 18:22).

"For what [are we] worth?" (Isa 2:22). We are worth the image and likeness of God. That is our glory, and it is a weight we can take with us!

QUESTIONS FOR YOUR REFLECTION

1. What are your thoughts on this? What carries a lot of weight with me is who I shall become. Read Psalm 115.

2. How would you explain the kinship between poverty of spirit and the glory of God?

3. Evidences of quantitative religion can be found in the language with which we speak of religion, to wit: "Getting more grace," "receiving the sacraments," "getting my prayers said," "going to confession," and "getting Mass in," just to mention a few. What are nonquantitative ways of expressing religion's realities?

4. Read the "Martha and Mary" story in St. Luke's Gospel (10:38-42). In what way did Jesus gently chide quantitative religion?

WEDNESDAY OF THE FIRST WEEK

God Is Everywhere: Does It Make a Difference?

WORD

"Let me now sing a song of my friend,
my friend's song concerning his vineyard.
My friend had a vineyard
on a fertile hillside;
He spaded it, cleared it of stones,
and planted the choicest vines;
Within it he built a watchtower,
and hewed out a wine press.
Then he looked for the crop of grapes,
but what it yielded was wild grapes.

17

Now, inhabitants of Jerusalem and men of Judah,
  judge between me and my vineyard:
What more was there to do for my vineyard
  that I had not done?
Why, when I looked for the crop of grapes,
  did it bring forth wild grapes?" (Isa 5:1-4)

REFLECTION

Bursting with exuberance, a little girl ran toward her visiting neighbor and exclaimed, "Guess what I heard in church this morning?" With feigned astonishment the visitor replied, "For heaven's sake, Beth, tell me what you heard in church this morning!"

With outstretched arms, the child shouted, "God is in the world!"

"Wonderful news," acknowledged the guest, "but I have even better news."

The child's exuberance changed to curiosity. "What better news?" she asked.

Laying his hand on her head, the neighbor said gently, "God is in this room, in you, and in all of us."

The child glanced furtively at the other guests. After a few pensive moments, she approached a visiting priest and asked, "Is he telling the truth?"

With simplicity the priest answered, "He is."

Walking back reflectively to the neighbor, the little girl spoke quietly: "That makes things different, doesn't it?"

God is Immanuel—God is with us. Indeed, that "makes things different." The child's comment revealed an interesting reason why many people prefer God's presence in heaven rather than God's presence on earth. The more God can be kept in heaven the less involved people need to become with God's presence on earth. If God is with us—Immanuel—"that makes things different, doesn't it?"

God's presence in all of creation gives Advent a third dimension. We rob Advent of its fullest meaning when we confine it to the dimensions of Christ's past and future comings. Advent heralds a third coming, which invites us to look for Christ's presence *now,* a presence whose grandeur fills the whole world. St. Bernard of Clairvaux writes:

> We know that there are three comings of the Lord. The third lies
> in between the other two. It is invisible, while the other two are

visible. In the first coming he was seen on earth dwelling among men. . . . In the final coming . . . he will be seen in glory and majesty. The intermediate coming is a hidden one; in it only the elect see the Lord within their own selves, and they are saved.[3]

If we accept St. Bernard's third dimension of Christ's advent, we can more clearly understand Isaiah's parable of the vineyard bearing only wild grapes. His parable is of a vineyard lovingly attended to, deprived of nothing that guarantees the choicest fruit: "a fertile hillside . . . spaded . . . cleared of stones . . . the choicest vines . . . a watch-tower . . . a wine press . . . . What more was there to do for my vine-yard . . . ?"

Isaiah did not answer the question because the question was really the answer. There was nothing more the vinedresser could do for his vineyard because he had lavished it with total love. The whole vine-yard, unfortunately, elected not to respond to his daily coming. That is why it gave back only wild grapes.

Hidden beneath the story line of Isaiah's parable was a truth that makes a difference for all of us. Isaiah pleaded with his listeners to em-brace this truth, whose implications could change their lives:

> The vineyard of the LORD of hosts is the house of Israel,
>   and the men of Judah are his cherished plant;
> He looked for judgment, but see, bloodshed!
>   for justice, but hark, the outcry! (Isa 5:7)

Judgment is evidence. When God looked for judgment in the vine-yard of the elect there appeared only bloodshed and outcry, not the evidence of justice. The vineyard of the Lord yielded only wild grapes not because God punished the elect but because they elected not to respond to God's loving husbandry.

And so it is with us. God is our judgment because we were created to bear fruit that reveals us to be radically different from the rest of creation. God created humankind to be like God, and it is that purpose of human existence that compels God to be with us. This is the advent of Christ that invisibly stands between both of the visible comings of Christ—Christ in Bethlehem and Christ in majesty at the end of time. When we refuse to discern Christ's invisible comings with the eyes of faith, our lives bear only "wild grapes."

Our embrace of Immanuel—Christ with us—makes all the difference in the world. This was the exquisite insight that drew from the little girl God's choicest fruits of wonder and awe.

QUESTIONS FOR YOUR REFLECTION

1. How is human life different if it is lived from the perspective that God is with us?

2. Why is religion more comfortable when we keep God in heaven?

3. If we see God as "out there" rather than "with us," what difference does our perspective make in how we define faith? If God dwells in us, what does faith involve?

4. If judgment is the evidence of our response to God's loving care among us, does the evidence of "wild grapes" mean God's condemnation? Or is the evidence of "wild grapes" in our lives a sign that we have chosen not to respond to God's care for us?

THURSDAY OF THE FIRST WEEK

Waiting and Longing Are Spouses

WORD

> "To prevent his disciples from asking the time of his coming, Christ said: 'About that hour no one knows, neither the angels nor the Son. It is not for you to know times or moments.' He has kept all these things hidden so that we may keep watch, each of us thinking that he will come in our own day. If he had revealed the time of his coming, his coming would have lost its savor: it would no longer be an object of yearning for the nations and the age in which it will be revealed" (St. Ephrem, deacon).[4]

REFLECTION

Although I knew little of the Book of Job when I was sixteen, I unwittingly experienced the meaning of his story on one unforgettable occasion, as I watched my 53-year-old father sobbing at our family table. Completely bent over, he was the picture of helplessness, as he endeavored to cope with the sudden news that his job of 23 years had been terminated. He joined millions whose job terminations without unemployment benefits offered them no more than the Job experience of family poverty and ego demolition.

While prayer was a significant part of my adolescent life, my father's predicament began a two-year encounter with prayer I have yet to match. I frequently recall those two years of storming heaven with cries of petition for my father's intention. Daily Mass, visits to the high-school chapel, frequent visits to our parish church, and long encounters with God as I walked the two-mile journey to and from school became a major part of my routine.

During those two years of waiting while God seemed not to be listening, I persisted because of a remark made by a religion teacher: "If your prayer is rooted in a hope which is no more than a pious wish, then your prayer is like placing a bet on a horse." This remark sparked my resolution to persevere, and in due time I began to understand that waiting is the prelude to hope. The more persistently I prayed, the more I perceived hope to be certainty rather than the prelude of wishful thinking for racetrack success.

After two years of prayer and waiting, my father finally secured a good job, which he held until his death 14 years later. My Job experience ended, but it left an indelible and fruitful mark on my spirit. I began to realize that waiting, prayerfully encountered, had expanded my interior life to embrace more fully the presence of God that I was created and baptized to encounter. Evidence of that interior expansion was the appearance of a longing to serve God and the Church. This was the longing that attracted me to the priesthood, whose way of life I joyfully embraced ten years after my Job experience.

I rarely begin Advent without recalling this experience, for therein lies much of Advent's significance. Advent is about waiting and longing. They are spouses. It is in waiting that there is uncovered the priceless gift of longing. Together they take us beneath the surface of our egos into the uncharted expanses of our interior lives, where birth of a fuller selfhood is a certainty. This descent takes time, but the discovery of who God meant us to be—God's image and likeness—is worth the parenthood of waiting and longing.

This is not to condemn the ego satisfaction that arises from genuine self-knowledge. Ego is not always the imagination of what one's identity is. Who I know myself to be is healthy ego. Ego becomes unhealthy when one concludes that ego is the totality of one's identity. When we conclude that there cannot possibly be further dimensions of our personhood, the healthy longing to enter the vast regions of hidden "moreness" is silenced, and human growth ends.

Those who perceive their egos to be the wholeness of identity easily become impatient people. Why wait? becomes the centerpiece question of their lives. If one's identity is perceived to be final, why wait for anything? Isn't this the question that undergirds much of today's marketing practices? The throwaway feature of today's products with their built-in obsolescence is evidence that among millions of people instant gratification is an imperative. Our longings become addicted to instant indulgence, evidence of the loathing we have for anything that requires waiting.

Aren't we more than the ego we experience? Certainly! Yet if ego identity is regarded as identity's finality, then it becomes difficult to grasp the biblical truth that humanity has been created to be like God, in whom there is no other finality of definition. God's image and our likeness to that image call us to transcend the boundaries of ego knowledge.

God created us with a capacity to share in the infinite expanse of God's mystery, where finality of identity other than God's presence does not exist. Lying within the depths of who we are is a never-ending moreness, accompanied with God's gift of hope to make us persistent and patient as we await hope's certainty. God invites us to wait, so that from waiting's agony the gift of longing for the moreness of who we are might be revealed. How beautifully the psalmist voices this Advent perspective:

> Commit to the LORD your way;
> > trust in him, and he will act.
> He will make justice dawn for you like the light;
> > bright as the noonday shall be your vindication.
>
> Leave it to the LORD,
> > and wait for him; . . . (Ps 37:5-7).

QUESTIONS FOR YOUR REFLECTION

1. What is the difference between the ego of knowing who you are and the ego that borrows its ego knowledge from marketing's fantasy?

2. Why is impatience the fruit of the conviction that one's ego knowledge is total identity?

3. Why does awareness of our moreness motivate us to be patient?

4. It doesn't seem to occur to egocentric people that God is more than they understand God to be. Is that why Advent's spirituality calls us to embrace the spirituality of waiting and longing?

Finding God in Exile

WORD

"Lord, my God, teach my heart where and how to seek you, where and how to find you. Lord, if you are not here where shall I look for you in your absence? Yet if you are everywhere, why do I not see you when you are present?" (St. Anselm, bishop).[5]

REFLECTION

"I have had an experience of God" is a disclosure to which I give cautious attention. My caution is due not to doubts about the possibility of experiencing God but about the possibility that the alleged experiences of God might really be human experiences of self. Discerning the difference between these two possibilities can be a fruitful Advent exercise.

It is interesting that when St. Anselm prays for an advent of God into his life, he pictures himself an exile. Speaking first to himself he cries out: "Insignificant man, escape from your everyday business for a short while, hide for a moment from your restless thoughts. Break off from your cares and troubles and be less concerned about your tasks and labors. Make a little time for God and rest a while in him."[6]

Turning to God, St. Anselm continues:

Lord most high, what shall this exile do, so far from you? What shall your servant do, tormented by love of you and cast so far

23

from your face? He yearns to see you, and your face is too far from him. He desires to approach you, and your dwelling is unapproachable. He longs to find you, and does not know your dwelling place. He strives to look for you, and does not know your face.[7]

St. Anselm's prayer embodies a criterion with which we can discern between human experience of self and faith experience of God. This criterion is a deep longing for God—a longing that accompanies a felt impossibility of achieving the experience of God's presence. In short, a deep hunger and thirst to experience God is itself an experience of God. Our longings for God are evidence that God is infinitely more than we can humanly embrace. The experience of exile moves us to authentic faith, whereby we encounter God. Human feelings of impossibility make straight the way of faith with its capacity to put us in touch with God.

The theme of a small book that I read many years ago maintains that the search for Christ is the finding of Christ. As I read the book, my initial puzzlement gave way to the joyful understanding of its Advent theme of longing. Advent proclaims a coming of Christ not from a state of his absence but from a state of our earthly incapacity to experience his presence in our midst. The surest sign that Christ comes is the paradoxical reality that we are always longing and searching for his presence. The fact that we long and search for a presence beyond our human capacity to experience is evidence that we are encountering God. When we confidently assert what bumper stickers proclaim, "I found it," we become losers.

If "I found it" is life's goal, there is little need for faith and hope. These virtues are God's precious gifts of enablement, whereby we can reach beyond our human capacity to touch God's moreness. Graced with faith and hope, we possess the possibility of experiencing here upon earth what God created us to become—the likeness to God's image. We experience only ourselves when we imagine an experience of God solely on the basis of our human feelings. These earthly measurements give us only an illusion of experiencing God.

Human life has the nature of pilgrimage and search. Graced with faith and hope, our search and longing for God is our experience of God. Why? Because human nature's God-given purpose can never be fully found in this life. There is always more. Look at the lives of the saints. They reveal not one shred of evidence of an "I found it" spirituality. Quite to the contrary, the lives of the saints gave evidence of a spirituality of longing. The more God's holiness unfolded, the more they experienced exile from God's presence. The further away God seemed to be, the more intense became their prayer of longing. They no longer lived under the illusion that God could be found solely by human prowess.

St. Anselm writes: "Teach me to seek you, and when I seek you show yourself to me, for I cannot seek you unless you teach me, nor can I find you unless you show yourself. Let me seek you in desiring you and desire you in seeking you, find you in loving you and love you in finding you."[8]

God's coming can be more fully understood within an ecclesial frame of reference. Our belonging to the Church must of necessity be centered in mission and pilgrimage because the Church is always in search of God's wholeness. The center of that wholeness is the Good Shepherd, who went in search of one lost sheep (see Luke 15:4-7). The 99 he left behind were also lost not because the shepherd was in ignorance of where they were but because the wholeness of their "flockship" was incomplete. As long as one sheep was lost, the wholeness of the flock was no longer intact. The flock could no longer be flock without the finding of the one lost sheep. It was only when the *lost* was found that the 99 *found* were no longer lost.

Lostness, like longing, is also a prelude to a genuine experience of God. Within the framework of our ecclesial passage toward the fuller embrace of God's moreness, we can expect a true experience of God. Our belonging to the Church can never be measured by a conviction that a static perception of who God is, what the Church is, and what orthodoxy is, is the final word about each. To be assured of God's never-ending presence demands of us that we leave what we have personally experienced of God so that our ecclesial belonging might provide us with the deeper experience of God's inexhaustible moreness in the wholeness of the flock. Those who are convinced that they have "found it" and no longer search for ecclesial dimensions of Christ's identity may be lost to a Church whose shepherds lead us in search of "flockship."

QUESTIONS FOR YOUR REFLECTION

1. To be lost is an "exile experience" where we find ourselves bereft of everything that provides us with earthly security. In what sense is exile—lostness—an experience of God? In what way is our exile experience a necessary condition for an advent experience?

2. In light of the meaning of "incarnation," why will our experience of God in heaven also be a genuine experience of self? What is the connection between Christ's incarnation and God's purpose for human existence?

3. "Apparitional spirituality" represents a longing to encounter heaven's inhabitants in the same way we encounter the inhabitants of this world. Is there a reason to be cautious of such experiences? Is there a possibility that apparitional spirituality might compromise faith? How?

4. Have you ever felt that you were losing your faith? Is it possible that this sense of loss was but the birth pangs of a genuine faith experience of God's moreness?

Longing for Belonging

WORD

>"Go, station a watchman,
>   let him tell what he sees.
>If he sees a chariot,
>   a pair of horses,
>Someone riding an ass,
>   someone riding a camel,
>Then let him pay heed,
>   very close heed.
>Then the watchman cried,
>'On the watchtower, O my Lord,
>   I stand constantly by day;
>And I stay at my post
>   through all the watches of the night'" (Isa 21:6-8).

REFLECTION

Patience is often an unhappy experience. Why? Because its endurance is perceived to be an inevitable fate rather than an integral part of human growth and development.

Unfortunately, patience understood solely as endurance keeps the door to Advent's fullest meaning closed. But patience as an integral part of human growth and development is Isaiah's "watchman," whose voice Advent echoes at the beginning of each Church year. "I stand constantly by day; And . . . through all the watches of the night."

The practice of patience is fruitless to the extent that we divorce it from the maturing process that enables us to behold the unfolding of Christ's presence in our lives. Patience is not a "necessary evil," to be endured until salvation rescues us from its ordeal. St. Cyprian writes, "Patience is a precept for salvation."[9] Patience is not a "ball-and-chains" existence, stalking us as we journey toward salvation; it is the journey.

Hope is salvation's indwelling presence within the womb of human development. As our human be-ing develops, we allow the "not yet" reality of hope's promise to become the reality of hope's promised fulfillment. This reality is Jesus Christ's ongoing incarnation—his becoming and his belonging to our humanity. This ongoing incarnation of Christ asks only for patience. We have Christ's word for the necessity of patience: "Know that I am with you always, until the end of the world" (Matt 28:20). St. Paul voices our own word: "If we hope for what we do not see, we wait for it in patience" (see Rom 8:25).

Thus St. Paul suggests why patience can become a trying virtue: "We hope for what we do not see, . . ." Patience stands at the midway point in human existence, where the needs of humanity's earthly existence meet the needs of God's higher existence. God created humanity to *become* that existence rather than to see it as we see this earth's realities all around us.

God created us for a destiny this world's "hope" cannot touch. God created us to *become* what we can't see rather than to *have* the possessions we can see. Life on earth, lived with God's gift of hope, is the midpoint of human existence. Patience enables us to make this life's short journey toward the perfection we were created to become and to which we were created to belong. Patience prepares us to embody the glory of salvation but delays while it makes us ready to *have* its fullest *being*.

At the core of patience there is one basic and universal suffering. Our lives here upon earth are lives of exile because we were not created to belong here forever. This world's lifetime of not-belonging keeps alive a never-ending longing, whose full satisfaction here on earth is simply not attainable. Salvation is not primarily about having this world's goods. Salvation is a longing for the belonging to eternal life, which only faith can touch while we live here upon earth.

On one occasion the word "salvation" became the focus of a children's group discussion I was conducting. In order to get to the meaning of salvation, I asked, "What does the word 'save' mean to you?" I received a variety of responses.

"My brother saved our cat from drowning in the pond last summer."

"When our house caught fire, my dad saved the TV set." (With amusement I wondered how Dad's wife and children fared.)

"My mother saves coupons."

"I'm saving money to buy a bicycle."

Amidst an avalanche of examples I began to wind down this somewhat humorous exercise of defining salvation. I could not, however, spurn a very small child who had been waving his hand, trying desperately to get my attention. Thank God I did let him get my attention!

"Salvation," he fairly shouted, "is putting things back where they belong!"

"What do you mean?" I asked, as I saw tremendous biblical and theological implications in what turned out to be his very unbiblical and untheological response.

"Well," he explained, "my mother tells us, 'Put your clothes where they belong tonight and you'll be my salvation tomorrow morning!' "

For me, the child's answer, viewed from a biblical and theological perspective, opened the door to the unfathomable riches of a salvation where longing for humanity's ultimate purpose of be-longing makes patience a cherished "having" and, above all, a lifetime vocation of watchful waiting.

In light of the little boy's response, might patience and its waiting be a much happier experience?

QUESTIONS FOR YOUR REFLECTION

1. If Christ has already come into the world and remains through the presence of the Holy Spirit, why does the Church persist in speaking about Christ's coming and the virtue of patience as a way of making us ready for his coming?

2. Can you relate the little boy's description of salvation ("putting things where they belong") to forgiveness, healing, reconciliation, and peacemaking? Do they take time? Aren't they the "makings" of salvation?

3. If "incarnation" means God's becoming human, can you connect human development with the continuing process of Christ's incarnation? Did it end or begin in Bethlehem?

4. Why is instant consumerism a danger to God's gift of hope and the patience that is its "watchman"?

5. Why is American society's instant-gratification obsession a major obstacle to the unfolding of Christ's incarnation in our humanity?

SECOND SUNDAY OF ADVENT

The Desert Is Hope's Home

WORD

> *"On that day you looked to the weapons in the House of the Forest; you saw that the breaches in the City of David were many; you collected the water of the lower pool. You numbered the houses of Jerusalem, tearing some down to strengthen the wall; you made a reservoir between the two walls for the water of the old pool. But you did not look to the city's Maker, nor did you consider him who built it long ago"* (Isa 22:8-12).

REFLECTION

These words are from an angry Isaiah. His anger was not about the people's liberation from the savagery of Assyrian captivity. Isaiah was angry because the liberated threw themselves into the restoration of Jerusalem without any thought of the Maker for whom Jerusalem was the symbol. Isaiah regarded God's merciful liberation as the call to renew an ancient covenant between themselves and their Lord:

> On that day the Lord,
> > the GOD of hosts, called on you
> To weep and mourn,
> > to shave your head and put on sackcloth.
> But look! You feast and celebrate,
> > you slaughter oxen and butcher sheep,
> You eat meat and drink wine [saying]:
> "Eat and drink, for tomorrow we die!" (Isa 22:12-13)

Isaiah's angry words revolved around an inconsistency between restored symbols and the people's failure to live the reality of their covenant meaning. He deemed it inconsistent for them to celebrate the restoration of breached symbols without the intention of restoring the breaches of covenant between themselves and God.

This is an important Advent theme. Advent begins the Church's year by insisting that no coming of Christ can be experienced *solely* on the level of refurbished externals. Jesus will never be found in a desert of broken externals without there being the intention of restoring broken covenanted relationships. Jesus will always be found in desert experiences where he finds repentance and its corresponding commitment to heal broken hearts.

We can more clearly understand the meaning of Advent when we grasp its connection with the biblical theme of desert. From the "formless wasteland" from which God began creation (see Gen 1:1) until Jesus' wasteland experience on the cross from which God raised Jesus from the jaws of death, the desert experience calls again and again from the pages of God's Word. Eusebius of Caesarea comments on Isaiah's plea:

> A voice cries out:
> In the desert prepare the way of the LORD!
> Make straight in the wasteland a highway for our God (Isa 40:3).

Eusebius writes: "The prophecy makes clear that it is to be fulfilled, not in Jerusalem but in the wilderness: it is there that this glory of the Lord is to appear, and God's salvation is to be made known to all mankind."[10]

Christ's way into the lives of the Israelites was not made straight simply because of the historical evidence of liberation. Isaiah pleaded with the liberated to see what God saw—evidence of unrepented breaches between themselves and God. Isaiah exercised the prophetic role of discerning the evidence of inconsistency. He called the inconsistent to choose repentance as their reason for celebration. Isaiah was angry because people were repairing once-abandoned walls when it was an abandoned covenant oneness they should have been restoring.

Repentance is authentic when we experience its stirrings in desert experiences like helplessness, poverty, and utter dependence. The desert is God's highway into our lives. The truly repentant person abandons created means as the way to the presence of God. In desert experiences, no way to God is open except Christ, who stands ready to share our deserts. That's good news!

Advent calls us to embrace our desert experiences. These are where hope, not despair, is nourished. No matter how tragic a desert experience, how empty one's life, how bereft one is of this world's securities, the wilderness experience—oh, happy paradox—contains the certainty of God's gift of hope. The certainty? Jesus himself began his mission in deserts! It was in these desert experiences that the Father cried out: "This is my beloved Son. My favor rests on him" (Matt 3:17).

It was in the desert that God offered us the good news of a new creation, Jesus Christ. Jesus came not as the restoration of the old Jerusalem but as a completely new Jerusalem. It was as such that Jesus made his way to the old Jerusalem where his death on the cross became the final wasteland, out of which God began a new creation, Christ's resurrection!

Advent's joy has its source in this world's tears. In our tears we cry out, "My God, my God, why have you forsaken me?" (Matt 27:46) Advent's joy amidst our tears is the certainty of hope—God has come! The desert of our own forsakenness with the tears of our utter helplessness is *the way* God has chosen to come to us. God begs us to travel that straight way and come to Christ.

QUESTIONS FOR YOUR REFLECTION

1. Recall symbols you frequently or regularly use. Do you sometimes surmise an inconsistency between their routine performance and the lived reality they symbolize? Give an example.

2. Words like "void," "emptiness," and "poverty" characterize the meaning of desert. How do you associate these meanings with Advent and its never-ending theme of hope?

3. For many people, fasting is a symbol of giving up something, a gesture to indicate the desire to make up for past transgressions. Doesn't fasting, however, call us to look into deeper deserts of inconsistency between what we say we believe and how we live what we say? Shouldn't fasts give us hungers and thirsts for stronger relationships with God and those we love?

4. Call to mind desert experiences in your own life that you now concede have been blessings. Can you identify an advent of God into your life as the fruit of those experiences?

Comings Never Dreamed Possible

WORD

> "Lo, the LORD empties the land and lays it waste;
>   he turns it upside down,
>   scattering its inhabitants:
> Layman and priest alike,
>   servant and master,
> The maid as her mistress,
>   the buyer as the seller,
> The lender as the borrower,
>   the creditor as the debtor.
> The earth is utterly laid waste, utterly stripped,
>   for the LORD has decreed this thing" (Isa 24:1-3).

REFLECTION

Advent proclaims a coming of God never dreamed possible. Advent is about comings of God, whose ongoing revelation is from sources beyond our capacity to imagine. This does not mean that our images of God have not served a saving purpose in our lives. But Advent insists that God is always more than we have imagined and invites us to welcome salvific comings of God we have never dreamed possible. The desert experiences of our lives lead us to levels of God-consciousness that enhance our capacities to experience God. Those who endeavor to stand before God with rigid perceptions of God's identity are in danger of making their rigidity the god of their own making. The desert experiences of our lives are blessings because they invite us to abandon gods who fail us in the wastelands of our lives. The presence of God—He-who-is-to-come—in our wasteland experiences is certain because "the LORD has decreed this thing."

In the recent past, I suddenly found myself in a wasteland experience. I suffered a paralyzing stroke. For me, "The earth [was] utterly laid waste, utterly stripped." It happened in Advent.

During most of the day, I received many examinations followed by lengthy waiting periods. I used the time to pray. As I gazed at my disfigured hand and weighed the terrible implications of a lifeless right side for the rest of my life, I envisioned enormous changes. I felt helpless.

While my life seemed no longer intact, I still found my freedom intact. At no time before had I experienced hope's certainty as I did during those moments of prayerful reflection. I found myself challenging God with the certainty of hope to show me a way of following Christ in an utterly new way, paralysis notwithstanding.

Gazing at my lifeless right side, I made an act of faith on the cross of my helplessness in the presence of Christ. From that desert experience, I asked God to raise up for me a new way of following Jesus. Certainty that God would respond characterized my petition, even though there was no image of what my future would be.

After many examinations I was taken to intensive care, where, mercifully, I fell into deep sleep. When I awakened, I was astonished to find no more disfigurement or paralysis. With amazement I discovered that I could move both the arm and the leg, even sit up in bed. When the doctors and nurses came into the room, they found me walking toward the door. They stood speechless!

The restoration of my physical powers has been a source of never-ending joy to me. As wondrous as this deed was, still, it *was* within my limited capacity to see its relationship to God as healer. What startled my imagination, however, was the possibility of God's intervention in *my* life. My imagination could cope with the miracle of full healing in the lives of others. But mine? It was beyond my capacity to imagine it.

33

The word of God is much more than a listing of God's wonders in the lives of others. These amaze us, but they fit our image of God. They serve a saving purpose when they beckon us to travel inwardly to where Christ longs to meet us at the points of our brokenness, where we may hear Christ the healer say to us: "I do will it. Be cured" (Luke 5:13). Oh, the miracle to have the imagination to envision God's eagerness to touch our own lives! Our inward brokenness is the wasteland where God is ready to begin a new creation in us. Beyond our capacity even to dream of wasteland's possibilities, God's new creation is the transformation of our lives, in which the image and likeness of God—holiness—becomes a reality, a coming we never dreamed possible.

Advent spirituality invites us to open ourselves to expectations as humanly impossible to imagine as it is divinely certain that Christ is waiting for us in the wastelands of our brokenness. Advent challenges us to fix our eyes on Jesus, who dwells in the wastelands of poverty we imagine to be unfit for divine presence. If we find the challenge unacceptable and impossible, then we shall forever be ignorant of genuine hope. Advent invites us to the crux of Advent spirituality, that is, to travel the highway of hope leading beyond the parameters of our imagined expectations to the land of unimagined certainty, where Christ dwells in the deserts of our brokenness.

God's gift of hope calls us to fix our eyes on the whole Christ—both the Christ we have experienced and the Christ we have not. The straightest way we come to Christ is not in the fixed image we have of God. Rather, it is in the "near-despair" moments of our lives, where impossibility seems to be the finality of our earthly expectations. Here God's gift of hope offers us the certainty of Christ's readiness to meet us with a presence we never imagined.

Miracles are not what Christ offers our eyes to perceive; miracles are what Christ offers our minds and hearts to believe. Miracles invite us to believe that companionship with Christ in the wastelands of our lives is certain. "God could then answer," writes St. John of the Cross, " 'This is my beloved Son in whom I am well pleased; hear him.' . . . Fix your eyes on him alone for in him you will find more than you could ever ask for or desire."[11]

QUESTIONS FOR YOUR REFLECTION

1. Are miracles contradictions of reality or are they revelations of the God whose being exceeds our image of God?

2. Wasteland experiences sometimes evoke the response, what did I ever do to deserve this? What marvelous opportunity do people miss when their reaction to affliction is a question about their unworthiness?

3. Why can Christ's presence be more certain in times of affliction than in times of well being that easily fit our image of his presence?

4. If your prayers have not resulted in the alleviation of a cross, has God nevertheless come to you in ways that exceeded your capacity to imagine?

The Church: Sacrament of Healthy Tension

WORD

"O LORD, you are my God,
  I will extol you and praise your name;
For you have fulfilled your wonderful plans of old,
  faithful and true.
For you have made the city a heap,
  the fortified city a ruin;
The castle of the insolent is a city no more,
  nor ever to be rebuilt.
Therefore a strong people will honor you,
  fierce nations will fear you.
For you are a refuge to the poor,
  a refuge to the needy in distress;
Shelter from the rain,
  shade from the heat.
As with the cold rain,
  as with the desert heat,
  even so you quell the uproar of the wanton" (Isa 25:1-5).

REFLECTION

At all times the Church is in tension. On the one hand, faith moves her to extol and praise God for "wonderful plans of old, faithful and true," and on the other, she struggles to offer good news to a city of imperfections, "a heap . . . a ruin . . . [never] to be rebuilt." It is in this tension of perfection and imperfection that the Church proclaims the certainty of Advent's hope.

The Church is unique because she is a sacrament of this tension. At all times she embodies the perfection of Christ, along with the imperfections of those who constitute his mystical body. Indeed, this embodied tension is the Church's identity.

This is the Church's sacramentality, which the Fathers of the Second Vatican Council refer to when they write:

> Lifted above the earth, Christ drew all things to himself. Rising from the dead, he sent his life-giving Spirit upon his disciples, and through the Spirit established his Body, which is the Church, as the universal sacrament of salvation. Seated at the right hand of the Father, he works unceasingly in the world, to draw men [and women] into the Church and through it to join them more closely to himself, nourishing them with his own body and blood, and so making them share in his life of glory.[12]

The Church is perfect insofar as her union with Christ is the coming reality of her identity; the Church is imperfect insofar as Christ's holiness among imperfect and sinful members has not yet fully come. The Church is perfect because she holds within her womb the fullness of Christ's identity; the Church is imperfect because her members have yet to allow full birth of Christ's identity.

Discipleship is authentic when the followers of Christ are faithful to the Church at the point of tension where the Church faces the ambiguity of her identity. Discipleship becomes questionable when evidences of human imperfection cause her members to settle for imperfection. Discipleship becomes unquestionable when imperfect disciples place their trust in the certainty that all men and women have been created to share the perfection of God's likeness. Disciples of Christ do not settle for imperfection!

Hope's certainty, then, enables imperfect Church members to reach out in human solidarity together with Christ to be instruments of healing, renewal, reconciliation, and forgiveness. The authenticity and strength of discipleship are not achievements worked out within the parameters of passivity of sinful members working in a sanitized, antiseptic, immunized "perfect society" of human institution. The authenticity and strength of discipleship are the longings of sinners to be

> . . . a refuge to the poor,
>   a refuge to the needy in distress;
> Shelter from the rain,
>   shade from the heat.
> As with the cold rain,
>   as with the desert heat,
>   even so you quell the uproar of the wanton (Isa 25:4-5).

Disciples who seriously expect the Church to achieve a Camelot existence here upon earth live under illusion. The work of salvation—healing, reconciliation, peacemaking, and forgiveness—is ongoing. God's spirit dwells in the Church to make Christ's advent a reality generation after generation. Yes, Christ is fully with us—Immanuel. The glory of God dwells fully within all of us. But it is a glory not yet fully realized. Why? Because we also bear the identity of this world's temporalities. Salvation is not an immunization from temporalities; it is a liberation from the illusion that this world's temporalities are the ultimate reasons for human existence.

There are no limits to a hope that promises to reach out to ever-deeper dimensions of Christ's presence. When we are not afraid to embrace the virtue of hope, Christ's presence visibly marks us with evidences of his identity. We have been graced to be witnesses to Christ's values, attitudes, priorities, aspirations, and longings. And while we can possess this identity of Christ, we never *fully* possess it because we are not God. We are children of God, whose identity we have been called to share. There is no end to God, and there is no end to the capacity we have to long for God's image, which we were created to share. And so it is with the Church. The Church will never be completely built because she always stands in need of witnesses whose unique gifts of holiness she has been called to mirror. In one of his memorable addresses, Pope Paul VI, commenting on Christ's words, "I will build my church" (Matt 16:18), writes:

> The words [I will build] indicate permanent action on the part of the Lord in regard to His Church. It indicates the dynamic character which the life of the Church, depicted as a building under construction, assumes. . . . It is always an incomplete building which

prolongs in temporal history its determined plan of accomplishment.[13]

The Church lives in the midst of the tension between the ideal of perfection God envisioned us to become and the unbecoming imperfection we too often prefer to sustain. It is at this point of tension we celebrate Advent. Advent calls us not only to celebrate Advent's past and future comings but also to celebrate Advent's coming *now*. May we gladly embrace a Church commissioned to reconcile what is already possible with what is not yet achieved!

QUESTIONS FOR YOUR REFLECTION

1. In light of the reflection, is there any such reality as perfect parish, perfect pastor, or perfect parishioner? Isn't it true that shopping around for any of the above is really the pursuit of illusion?

2. Along the same line of thought, how is Catholic "fundamentalism," with its insistence on "going back to fundamentals" inconsistent with Pope Paul VI's fundamental that the Church possesses the dynamic character of a building under construction?

3. Why is the mystery of Advent compatible with the perspective of Church as having the tension of an "already" perfection and a "not yet" imperfection?

4. Why is the term "pilgrim Church" an excellent way to describe Advent's "now" meaning?

A Time of Promise, a Time of Fulfillment

WORD

"On this mountain the LORD of hosts
will provide for all peoples
A feast of rich food and choice wines,
juicy, rich food and pure, choice wines.
On this mountain he will destroy
the veil that veils all peoples,
The web that is woven over all nations;
he will destroy death forever. . . .
On that day it will be said:
'Behold our God, to whom we looked to save us!
This is the LORD for whom we looked;
let us rejoice and be glad that he has saved us!' "

(Isa 25:6-9)

REFLECTION

St. Augustine writes: "God established a time for his promises and a time for their fulfillment."[14] Advent is the season that embodies both. It is about a coming fully present in Christ but unfulfilled while promise accompanies us on our journey toward growth and development.

The Christian life is a marriage between the promise of Christ's coming and its fulfillment in the lives of those called to be his living presence. It is like a wedded couple who solemnly vow to make real the oneness to which they consent. Nuptial integrity is the consistency between the oneness vowed sacramentally and the oneness made fully evident in the lived experience of the vows.

What is not seen on the wedding day is the hiddenness of that oneness down deep in each person's mystery. This is the oneness that weddings promise with certainty but need time to develop through experience. The vocation of marriage is the nuptial consent to call forth charisms that long for nuptial oneness. The mutual consent, "I do," con-

39

cludes the wedding; it also begins the marriage. Marriage is permanent—"unto death do us part"—because human personhood has no earthly measurements with which to define an identity created in the image and likeness of God. When the promise of marriage's consent is fulfilled in due time, nuptial oneness gives birth to the evidence of God's identity, the fulfillment of humanity's ultimate purpose.

Marriage enjoys the dignity of sacramentality because it represents more than the consent to live an earthly togetherness. Matrimony's sacredness signifies the yet-to-be advent of One who has already come but whose divine presence waits to be called forth from the deep recesses of matrimony's mutuality. When the calling forth of human personhood is clearly seen to be a nuptial priority, faith enables the married to see their role as participants in the ongoing incarnation of Christ, sent to be one with all of humanity. Matrimony is a sacrament because the faith of each person's "I do" is revealed in their solemn promise to call forth the hidden and "not yet" presence of Jesus Christ from the depths of each other's hidden presence. To ignore the sacramentality of matrimony's parenting of the never-ending coming of Christ's presence into our humanity is to practice worth control.

The sacrament of matrimony celebrates Advent's praise of oneness between Christ and his Church. Advent calls us to celebrate the beautiful truth that God's full glory already dwells within us but is yet to come. Advent invites us to remember the down-deep mystery of our personhood whose yet-to-come identity seeks the union of Christ's yet-to-come presence. The marriage of Christ and our humanity is permanent because the union of these espoused mysteries knows no end.

Is this a riddle? Yes, if faith is lacking, but no, if we respond with faith to climb Christ's mountain, upon which God promised with divinity's nuptial fidelity to "destroy the veil that veils all peoples, the web that is woven over all nations" (Isa 25:7). On this mountain, the Church, Advent calls us to live the tension between promise and fulfillment. Until Christ came, God's people lived by promise only. After his birth, God's people could live fully the reality of God's covenant. But now—this lifetime of Advent—we are called to live the tension between both.

Is there an impossible tension in the marriage of humanity and divinity, mortality and immortality, ordinary morality and holiness? Have we been created a "little less than the angels" (Ps 8:6), yet wedded to the destiny of sharing fully the glory of God along with the angels? Impossible? Not according to St. Augustine: "It was not enough for God to make his Son our guide to the way; he made him the way itself, that you might travel with him as leader, and by him as the way."[15]

Christ is not a road map, a contract, or a constitution. Christ is the organism of our lives, the principle of life by which we are on our way to the fulfillment of God's plan for human creation. To be wholly alive for the embrace of Christ's way is to follow the light that guides us safely through the times of promise to fulfillment. No wonder that St. Paul cries out, "For, to me, 'life' means Christ" (Phil 1:21).

QUESTIONS FOR YOUR REFLECTION

1. What are some examples from your life of something that has already come yet hasn't yet come?

2. What is the tension between mystery as hiddenness and mystery as unexplainability? How would you wed these two realities of mystery?

3. How would you explain the image of matrimony between Christ and the Church? When Jesus says "I do," to what is he consenting? When we say "I do," to what are we consenting?

4. What is the difference between Jesus as a "signpost" to heaven and Jesus as the "way" to heaven?

THURSDAY OF THE SECOND WEEK

Agape: *Senseless Love?*

WORD

"It is intolerable for love not to see the object of its longing. That is why whatever reward they merited was nothing to the saints if they could not see the Lord. A love that desires to see God may not have reasonableness on its side, but it is evidence of filial love" (St. Peter Chrysologus, bishop).[16]

REFLECTION

When compared with this world's version of love, authentic love appears to be utterly unreasonable, senseless, and "off the wall." When, however, we come to understand love's deepest meaning, its mystery, we must admit that unreasonableness is untrue of authentic love. Those who search for authentic love's deepest meaning run the risk of ridicule, but they surrender themselves to the creatorship of God, who longs to transform our creaturehood.

"God is love" (1 John 4:8). Love is not what God does; love is who God is! What God does is who God is. Our enactment of authentic love is indisputable evidence that God's created plan is wonderfully unfolding in our transformed lives—we are living in the image and likeness of God. God's gift of love is God's own self, grace-fully wedded to our gift of self.

An ancient word for authentic love is *agape*. This is the love that cries out, I love you for what I can be and do for you. This cry is the voice of God. It has the sound of authenticity, resonating God's identity in ours. Its voice rises above the cacophony of noises from this world's cry of love: "I love you for what you can do for me." This is the love that, when confronted with *agape* opts for the pleasure of this world's sense-ability rather than the joy of God's horizonless love-ability.

Agape does not spring from sense-ability. It arises from the sense-free depths of God's spirit-presence in the mystery of human identity. In the hiddenness of our mystery Christ calls out to us to unveil his presence in the humanity where Christ's ongoing incarnation never ceases being the plan of God. In every act of *agape*—unconditional love—there lies at its source the Beloved, beheld with the eyes of faith. Those who encounter *agape* without the eyes of faith condemn it from the ghetto of shallow perceptions of sense-filled love, beyond which they indict *agape* "senseless love."

What is the motivation for *agape*? It is the burning desire to see God, which "may not have reasonableness on its side, but . . . is evidence of filial love." Unreasonable and senseless as *agape* may appear, it unveils evidence of God's longing *to have us come* out of the ghettos of shallow love to embody a love only faith can "taste and see [to know] how good the LORD is" (Ps 34:9).

To love others far beyond expectations of earthly reward and remuneration is to cry out to the Beloved with the voice of blind Bartimaeus, "I want to see" (Mark 10:51). Here is the profoundest of all

42

longings urging us to look beyond the parameters of reason and sense. But the longing of *agape* is also the longing of God, whose Son "emptied himself and took the form of a slave . . . accepting even death, death on a cross" (Phil 2:7-8). *Agape* stands out above all other loves because it voices the longing of God thirsting for communion of God and humanity. *Agape* reveals itself in our own continuous thirst for a happiness impossible to be experienced in this world. With *agape*, the longings of God and humanity meet and are forever joined in the matrimony of God's covenant. In that wedding of weddings God and humankind become one in their longings.

We need to know that longing is not solely a human prerogative. We need to realize that God, too, longs—to reveal within us the full weight of God's glory. God longs for the advent of our surrender to the experience of heaven's glory on earth. But evidence of God's glory is not pleasure. It is "love, joy, peace, patient endurance, kindness, generosity, faith, mildness, and chastity" (Gal 5:22). To taste these fruits of the Spirit is to see God with the awareness of God's longing to be one with us. This is the experience that convinces us that no earthly remuneration matches heaven's fruitful evidences of humanity's taste of ultimate identity.

How do we "make straight in the wasteland a highway for our God" (Isa 40:3)? Faith in the "unreasonableness" of God's love! In the light of *agape* can we say, "O senseless father of the prodigal son"? Is he senseless because he welcomed home a son whose prodigality revealed itself in the wretchedness of his ingratitude, arrogance, and insolence (see Luke 15:11-32)? Was not the father's senseless love the straight highway for his repentant son's return to belonging? Was Jesus senseless to tell this story?

Agape is the love whose coming Advent proclaims. To love others beyond the point of reasonableness is no more unreasonable than to have the presence of Christ within us and to be unaware of his longing to love us as only God can love. To love others beyond reasonableness is to pray:

> My soul yearns for you in the night,
>   yes, my spirit within me keeps vigil for you;
> When your judgment dawns upon the earth,
>   the world's inhabitants learn justice. . . .
> See, the LORD goes forth from his place (Isa 26:9, 21).

QUESTIONS FOR YOUR REFLECTION

1. Why does God's love—*agape*—seem to be unreasonable?

2. What appears to you to be the "unreasonableness" of Christ's message? For example, how does the response of the elder son strike you (see Luke 15:25-32)? Was Christ unreasonable when he asked Peter to forgive "seventy times seven times" (Matt 18:22)? What are some other examples of "unreasonable" love?

3. Why is *agape* unlike any other love?

4. How do you think your life might be different if you more fully grasped that God too has longings? Would such an understanding gradually bring to an end our less-than-genuine longings?

FRIDAY OF THE SECOND WEEK

No Door Too Narrow for Human Dignity

WORD

"The Lord, coming into his own creation in visible form, was sustained by his own creation which he himself sustains in being. His obedience on the tree of the cross reversed the disobedience at the tree in Eden; the good news of the truth announced by an angel to Mary, a virgin subject to her husband, undid the evil lie that seduced Eve, a virgin espoused to a husband" (St. Irenaeus, bishop).[17]

REFLECTION

Contemporary architects design doors for baggage and people. In the time of Jesus, doors for the walls of cities were designed only for people. Today's demand for multipurpose doors designed for both baggage and people may be one reason why Jesus' "narrow door" for the "saved" seems quaint. "Try to come in through the narrow door. Many, I tell you, will try to enter and be unable" (Luke 13:24).

Narrow doors have no place in the imagination of moderns who demand wide doors for bulging baggage. In Jesus' time, however, narrow passageways deterred baggaged travelers. However quaint narrow doors seem to us, Jesus used that imagery to show that human dignity was the only baggage needed for clear passage through salvation's portals.

Salvation's door is not narrow because God chose only a few to be saved. It is narrow because human dignity asks only for space within the limitless expanses of human hearts. The door of salvation admits a human dignity created in the image and likeness of God. That's what we're worth, and no other "I.D." is required for salvation.

The good news of salvation does not arise out of what we possess as we knock on the door to eternal life. To define human personhood by what we have is to saddle it with a weight whose indignity is too cumbersome for salvation's narrow door. God created us to be defined by who God is, not by what we possess. We are God's children, sharing even more than human solidarity. We also share the communion of God's fatherhood and motherhood, of God's sonship in Christ, and of God's love in the Holy Spirit. This is the communion that identifies us and defines us. To approach salvation's judge at the end of our earthly pilgrimage with anything less than the radiance of God's glory is to carry a weight too cumbersome for passage through salvation's door.

Humankind's first sin was Eve's surrender to the serpent's lie that possession of God's earthly goods was the necessary credential for God-likeness. When Eve fell for that, she encumbered herself with baggage that replaced her God-given human dignity. She bought the lie that human dignity was defined by the baggage of this world's goods. Nothing of this world is required for our eternal happiness. No door is too narrow for the admittance of all men and women who possess the weight of God's glory as their reason for existence. Yes, you *can* take *that* with you!

What is the sign of this beautiful truth? Mary's virginity stands as silent testimony to human dignity's dependence for shape and form on that which is beyond the world's capacity to give humanity ultimate meaning. St. Irenaeus writes:

> As Eve was seduced by the word of an angel and so fled from God after disobeying his word, Mary in turn was given the good news by the word of an angel and bore God in obedience to his word. As Eve was seduced into disobedience to God, so Mary was per-

suaded into obedience to God . . . the Virgin Mary became the advocate of the virgin Eve.[18]

The tragedy of Eve's disobedience was her failure to accept God's word that her humanity possessed the God-given dignity to be like God. She believed the serpent's word that God's forbidden fruit possessed powers to make her like God. The fruit of the forbidden tree "of knowledge of good and bad" (Gen 2:17) was off limits not because of sovereign powers the serpent alleged it to possess. It was forbidden because its presence *among all other trees* signified its inability to grant the glory of eternal happiness.

Mary's virginity was not a denial of human sexuality's goodness. Her virginity signified God's word that beyond the goodness of sexuality there was yet to be born a goodness beyond sexuality's capacity to provide. Mary's virginal motherhood freed God to give testimony that for our ultimate happiness there exists a goodness this world has not the creatorship to bestow. Mary's virginity confronted the serpent's ongoing lie that beyond the fruitfulness of this earth no goodness exists.

Mary's virginity will forever stand as her obedience to God's word, whose sovereign power is not of this world's making. Her obedience to the word's transcendence enabled her to bear the fruit of her womb, Jesus. Mary's virginity offered God's fatherhood the freedom to overshadow Mary with the Holy Spirit (see Luke 1:35) and give birth to God's Son, Jesus. Clearly, this was a fruitfulness completely beyond human sexuality's power. Her virginal motherhood stands as a silent witness to human dignity's eternal worth in the eyes of God. When Mary surrendered her will to God's, she opened the door to the salvation that welcomes all whose only possession is God's gift of God-likeness. No door is too narrow for that worth.

QUESTIONS FOR YOUR REFLECTION

1. There is the saying, "You can't take it with you." Might this proverb be rooted in Jesus' advice, "Try to come in through the narrow door" (Luke 13:24)? How?

2. When Jesus said, "How blest are the poor in spirit" (Matt 5:3), was not this the "I.D." card for our admittance through the narrow door to salvation? How does "poor in spirit" relate to God's definition of human worth?

46

3. Is "virginal motherhood" a contradiction of terms? Without the virginity of Mary, would not God the Father have been limited to human sexuality's relationship to human fatherhood and motherhood? In what way did Mary's virginity leave God free to be God?

4. A beautiful Eucharistic hymn begins with the words "Look beyond." In what way is Mary's virginity Advent's ongoing invitation to look beyond this world's goodness for the yet-to-be-revealed goodness of God?

Sharing the Motherhood of Mary

WORD

"The Lord's inheritance is, in a general sense, the Church; in a special sense, Mary; in an individual sense, the Christian. Christ dwelt for nine months in the tabernacle of Mary's womb. He dwells until the end of time in the tabernacle of the Church's faith. He will dwell forever in the knowledge and love of each faithful soul" (Blessed Isaac Stella, abbot).[19]

REFLECTION

This excerpt from the sermon of Blessed Isaac Stella is a good example of the universality of Mary's motherhood. By universality I mean the immeasurable expanse of Christ's womblike dwelling place on this earth. It is narrow orthodoxy to exalt only the motherhood of Mary as the singular dwelling place for Christ's earthly advent presence. Mary's maternity stands as the sacrament of a motherhood found in the Church's faith and in the motherhood of each individual soul's knowledge and love.

A fundamental and essential part of Catholic faith and its orthodoxy is contained in the biblical text "I will set my dwelling among you" (Lev 26:11). Surely this dwelling includes Mary, the Church, and each indi-

47

vidual member of the Church. The participants of the Second Vatican Council bore witness to the universality of God's dwelling here upon earth when they rejected giving consideration to Mary apart from other considerations of ecclesial constitution. Instead, the Fathers of the Second Vatican Council included Mary as an integral part of the Dogmatic Constitution on the Church:

> In the bodily and spiritual glory which she possesses in heaven, the mother of Jesus continues in this present world as the image and first flowering of the Church as she is to be perfected in the world to come. Likewise, Mary shines forth on earth, until the day of the Lord shall come (see 2 Pet 3:10), as a sign of sure hope and solace for the pilgrim people of God.[20]

The inclusion of Mary within the constitution of the Church's identity does not diminish the exalted role of her motherhood. The significant gesture of integrating Mary, Church, and individuals draws the attention of all the followers of Christ to their own share in Mary's motherhood of Jesus. For if the Church is the sacrament of Christ's ongoing incarnation here upon earth, all who make up the membership of the Church share collectively and individually in the ongoing motherhood of Christ's unfolding advent.

The work of building the Church is never finished. In the realm of human nature, her continuous growth is in the hands of human giftedness, creativeness, and ingenuity. Claiming the identity of Christ's body, the Church cannot stand apart institutionally from the unfinished process of Christ's incarnation. Members of Christ's body, acknowledging the unfinished nature of the Church, take part in the continuous task of building the Church so that Christ's hidden sovereign presence might be gradually revealed.

But the Church is more than a human organization. She is also an organism. Her principle of life, Jesus Christ, dwells within the Church's womb. She is both mother and identity of Christ's presence, groaning in pain for Christ's ongoing advent. As each of us offers our own individual capacity to share Mary's motherhood, we build the Church, enabling her to share with Mary the motherhood of Jesus.

It is imperative that we revive and renew a perspective of Marian motherhood that integrates Mary, Church, and individual into a trinity of motherhood. That triune maternity enables Christ to reign in a world yet to be in touch with his redemption. Mary is a model of motherhood not to be kept on a pedestal, far removed from our maternal participation in the advent of Christ. Her maternity has been God's sign of the universal motherhood that the Church, as body of Christ, has a right to claim and we, as members of the Church, can also rightly claim. Mary's maternity is real. The Church and each individual member of the Church never cease to give birth to God's Word, inviting all to embrace in knowledge, in faith, and in love Christ's power and presence.

Advent proclaims Mary not as the sole participant in the motherhood of Jesus' first coming. Advent clearly signals the virginal motherhood of Mary as the sign of Christ's *ecclesial* birth. The motherhood of Jesus did not cease when he was born in Bethlehem. Advent insists that Mary is a sign of the Church, the sacrament of the Church's virginal maternity. Mary's virginal motherhood is the indisputable assurance that the Church, in the overshadowing presence of the Holy Spirit, will never cease giving birth to Jesus as well as to those called to be in communion with Christ's life:

> The Church . . . contemplating Mary's mysterious sanctity, imitating her chastity, and fulfilling the Father's will, becomes herself a mother by accepting God's word in faith. For by her teaching and baptism she brings forth to a new and immortal life children who are conceived of the Holy Spirit and born of God. The Church herself is a virgin, who keeps whole and pure the fidelity she has pledged to her spouse. Imitating the Mother of her Lord, and by the power of the Holy Spirit, she preserves with virginal purity an integral faith, a firm hope, and a sincere charity.[21]

QUESTIONS FOR YOUR REFLECTION

1. Reflecting on our part in the ecclesial motherhood of Mary, do you think that, in the light of that truth, we might become instrumental in developing a deeper Marian devotion?

2. What are the implications of Mary's inclusion in the Second Vatican Council's document on the Church? How is Mary's motherhood enhanced rather than diminished?

3. How does Mary's motherhood enrich both human dignity and ecclesial dignity? Can you give specific examples of your own participation in Mary's motherhood? How is faith related to the Church's motherhood of Jesus?

4. Reflecting on the vowed celibacy of both religious and ordained, would you say that this way of life lends confusion to the Church's maternal role? Is Mary's virginal motherhood a contradiction? Is celibacy a contradiction?

THIRD SUNDAY OF ADVENT

Advent Calls Right from the Heart

WORD

> "The Lord said:
> Since this people draws near with words only
> and honors me with their lips alone,
> though their hearts are far from me,
> And their reverence for me has become
> routine observance of the precepts of men,
> Therefore I will again deal with this people
> in surprising and wondrous fashion: . . ." (Isa 29:13-14)

REFLECTION

Evangelization is jeopardized when the word of God is preached from the mind and not from the heart. When the word of God dwells only in the preacher's mind, it will enjoy little more than an acquaintanceship with the listener's heart. The preacher's voice which "draws near with words only" will fail to reach the heart, where God longs to transform the listener.

God's Word to humanity is not by words alone. The Word of God is the power and presence of God, spoken not only for the ears but also for the heart. Christ the Word, the power and presence of God, became fully human to enable all men and women to be the identity of God's power and presence. The Son of God came to dwell within the *hearts* of humankind forever! This beautiful truth changed the identity of St. Paul, who cried out, "For, to me, 'life' means Christ. . ." (Phil 1:21).

50

From deep within his heart Paul was persuaded that human existence without Christ was impossible. "Those things I used to consider gain I have now reappraised as loss in the light of Christ. I have come to rate all as loss in the light of the surpassing knowledge of my Lord Jesus Christ. . . . I have accounted all else rubbish so that Christ may be my wealth" (Phil 3:7-8).

Paul's surpassing knowledge of Jesus Christ was not an encyclopedic grasp of matters *about* Christ. Paul spoke from his heart, where Christ had grasped the totality of his personhood. For this reason, Christ's light, even to this day, enlightens all who welcome into their hearts Paul's heart-heard Word of God.

Evangelization is not the work of finely honed words about the gospel of Jesus. Evangelization is a heart-to-heart, identity-to-identity communication of the Word, whose power and presence transforms both the evangelized and the evangelizer. It is not so much a meeting of minds as it is a transformation of hearts, where dwells the heart of Christ.

Advent is the voice of evangelization crying out in a wasteland of values that offer us a human purpose as shallow as the identity of this world's perishable image and likeness. The Advent voice cries out, "Make straight in the wasteland a highway for our God!" (Isa 40:3) Advent's cry is for the conversion from this world's purpose of existence to that which God has implanted in the human heart.

The Word of God is not one of many values. It is *the* way, truth, and life of human purpose. The Word of God does not deny the value of this world's goods. It denies the central place with which we enshrine them in our hearts. The voice of this holy season invites us to a conversion whereby Christ and his kingdom—his way, his truth, and his life—will occupy the place of centrality in our hearts and in our identities. "Seek first [God's] kingship over you, his way of holiness, and all these things will be given you besides" (Matt 6:33).

In his apostolic exhortation "Evangelization in the Modern World," Pope Paul VI acknowledges conversion as the center of evangelization:

> The purpose of evangelization is . . . interior change, and if it had to be expressed in one sentence the best way of stating it would be to say that the Church evangelizes when she seeks to convert, solely through the divine power of the Message she proclaims, both the personal and collective consciences of the people, the activities in which they engage, and the lives and concrete milieux which are theirs.[22]

Conversion involves more than the inclusion of all geographic strata of humanity:

> For the Church, [transformation] is a question not only of preaching the Gospel in ever wider geographic areas or to ever greater numbers of people, but also of affecting and as it were, upsetting, through the power of the Gospel, mankind's criteria of judgment, determining values, points of interest, lines of thought, sources of inspiration and models of life, which are in contrast with the Word of God and the plan of salvation.[23]

Evangelization is not so much a matter of preaching words to nations as it is of calling the people of nations to enter their hearts to dethrone the centrality of this world's values, which have become their ultimate purpose of human existence. Evangelization must first be a transformation of hearts before it can be a conversion of nations.

Transformation of hearts challenges evangelizers to give witness to the power and presence of Christ's identity in the wholeness of their being. This is the witness that draws people near to God, not with words only but with the very identity of Christ, whose indwelling presence enjoys centrality in the hearts of evangelizers. It is from this centrality that Christ acts in a "surprising and wondrous fashion."

"Above all," writes Pope Paul VI,

> the Gospel must be proclaimed by witness. . . . Through this wordless witness . . . Christians stir up irresistible questions in the hearts of those who see how they live: Why are they like this? Why do they live in this way? What or who is it that inspires them? Why are they in our midst? Such a witness is already a silent proclamation of the Good News and a very effective one. Here we have an initial act of evangelization.[24]

QUESTIONS FOR YOUR REFLECTION

1. What is the difference between preaching and teaching? Which one seeks to form? Which one seeks to inform?

2. Pope Paul VI writes, "Modern man listens more willingly to witnesses than to teachers, and if he does listen to teachers, it is because they are witnesses."[25] Does this observation shed light on the proverb "Who you are speaks more loudly than what you say"?

3. In the biblical context, why is the human heart spoken of more often than the human mind? Which of the two is at the center of our human

identity? Which one searches for truth; which one searches for love? Can either be dispensed?

4. St. Paul uses the phrase, "speaking the truth in love" (see Eph 4:15). How would you explain this marriage of truth and love as the key to evangelization?

Waiting for What We Already Have

WORD

> "The LORD is waiting to show you favor,
>   and he rises to pity you;
> For the LORD is a God of justice:
>   blessed are all who wait for him!
> O People of Zion, who dwell in Jerusalem,
>   no more will you weep;
> He will be gracious to you when you cry out,
>   as soon as he hears he will answer you" (Isa 30:18-19).

REFLECTION

Why is there a waiting time before our prayers are answered? The answer to that question may be a surprise. The reason we wait for an answer to prayer is because God longs for the only prayer worth our human existence. God waits for us to cry out for the gift of serving God. That cry springs from a deep conviction that to serve God is the only reason we exist. God longs that we might long to serve only God, who is the image we were created to become.

Abbot William of St. Thierry prayed, "Truly you alone are the Lord. Your dominion is our salvation, for to serve you is nothing else but to be saved by you! O Lord, salvation is your gift and your blessing is upon your people; what else is your salvation but receiving from you the gift of loving you or being loved by you?"[26]

To be saved is to live according to God's purpose for human existence. This means that we serve God as God has served us. Jesus offered humankind the living image of servanthood that God truly is. The life of Jesus gives evidence that God has no other interest but the wholehearted service of humankind. Jesus revealed to humankind the ultimate image of God's love. He died on the cross that we might be rescued from an existence that is clearly beneath human dignity.

Basically, unhappiness is the fruit of the wholeheartedness we give to matters that miss the mark of human purpose. God waits for us to return to that mark. The return is the meaning of conversion. In addition, unhappiness comes from the illusion that happiness is service to values *we* have decided are ultimate. That's idolatry, and its tragedy is our conversion to its image and likeness. What we serve is what we become.

Anthony de Mello, S.J., in *The Song of the Bird,* tells about an eagle who spent his whole life missing the mark of eagle existence:

> A man found an eagle's egg and put it in the nest of a backyard hen. The eaglet hatched with the brood of chicks and grew up with them.
>
> All his life the eagle did what the backyard chickens did, thinking he was a backyard chicken. He scratched the earth for worms and insects. He clucked and cackled. And he would thrash his wings and fly a few feet into the air like the chickens. After all, that is how a chicken is supposed to fly, isn't it?
>
> Years passed and the eagle grew very old. One day he saw a magnificent bird far above him in the cloudless sky. It floated in graceful majesty among the powerful wind currents, with scarcely a beat of its strong golden wings.
>
> The old eagle looked on in awe. "Who's that?" he said to his neighbor.
>
> "That's the eagle, the king of the birds," said his neighbor. "But don't give it another thought. You and I are different from him."
>
> So the eagle never gave it another thought. He died thinking he was a backyard hen.[27]

The eagle missed the mark of eagle existence. He was created to soar in the skies with the eagles; he fell for the lie that he was no different from the chickens. The lie he fell for is the lie he became. And so it is with us. That we are content with the ego that never gives another thought to being a servant to God's purpose of human existence is why

God waits for us. He waits for us to wonder why our clucking egos can't fly with soaring eagles.

Why does Advent pray, "Come, Lord Jesus, come"? Why do we wait for God to come to us? We wait not because God hasn't come to us but because we don't realize that *God has come.* God waits for us to become aware that we have been created to be borne "up on eagle wings" (Exod 19:4).

QUESTIONS FOR YOUR REFLECTION

1. William of St. Thierry prayed, "Your dominion is our salvation." We usually do not connect dominion with salvation. In what way is God's dominion our salvation?

2. One meaning of "ruler" is "measure." In what way is rule—dominion—the measure of how we live our lives? What response do we make to God that will measure the fullness of our surrender to God's longing to be our servant? Give a name to that measurement.

3. Conversion is frequently perceived as "not sinning again." While that is a cherished ideal, is it the fullest meaning of conversion? To what does conversion invite us that we might live sinlessly according to God's rule of life?

4. Besides Christ's coming in Bethlehem and his coming at the end of time, there is also a coming of Christ already among us. Why is it that Christ seems not to have come?

Her Lowly Highness, Humility

WORD

"[God] reveals his secrets to a humble man and in his kindness invitingly draws that man to himself. When a humble man is brought to confusion, he experiences peace, because he stands firm in God and not in this world. Do not think that you have made any progress unless you feel that you are the lowest of all men" (The Imitation of Christ).[28]

REFLECTION

Humility is indispensible for growth in Christ. Contrary to the world's perception, however, humility's identity is not degradation. To feel base, sordid, and despicable as the pinnacle of humility is really "the pits." This perception of lowliness is not the meaning intended by the author of *The Imitation of Christ* when he writes, "Do not think that you have made any progress unless you feel that you are the lowest of all men."

The substance of humility is, above all, truth. God created humanity to share the exaltation of God's life—a vocation to a way of living that transcends all worldly patterns of living. These patterns are not of themselves evil, but they are not ultimate. Humility is an invitation to the truth that, transcending this world's good life, there is a life of goodness, that is, of becoming the purpose for which we have been created.

When the good life of this world becomes our ultimate pursuit, we lower ourselves beneath the God-given dignity of human existence, and we become the indignity this world deems to be the pinnacle of glory. Adam and Eve, tempted to the "heights" of the forbidden tree's glory, found only the pits of banishment from God's gift of grace.

When human vocation is perceived as no more than a call to have the goods of this world, their acquisition crowns disciples of the good life with a glory the world can weigh. This vocation emphasizes success in terms of one's ability to exercise a dominion of power that springs from possessions and accomplishments. In reality, it is a "lightweight" vocation because its pursuit is for the perishables of this world.

Who are the lowly in the eyes of those who champion the good life? They are the "inferiors" who have missed the mark of this world's ideals and values. They do not have an abundance of this world's goods, nor have they been able to accomplish feats of glory high on the list of this world's architects of self-esteem. Without any of this world's weight of glory, the "lowly" are far out on the periphery of this world's vision of glory.

Humility is a virtue that challenges this world's purpose of the human existence whose tightly drawn lines of identity exclude those who lack the world's credentials for belonging. Humility constantly calls us to a human purpose whose lines of definition mark who we are in the sight of God rather than what we possess in the eyes of the world. Humility reminds us of the truth that our "I am" shares God's "I AM" (see Exod 3:14). This world's rules for "discipleship" do not include God's I Am-ness as a credential for human dignity and belonging.

Humility's truth calls us to let go of any purpose of human existence that deafens us to God's secrets, blinds us to God's glory, and separates us from God's intimacy. Humility does not put us down; it raises us up to an understanding of the justice that judges us by the extent to which we reveal evidence of God's image and likeness. This is the justice we share with the "lowly," who lack the world's credentials for rubbing shoulders with the "highly."

The psalmist prays: "The Lord leads the humble to justice; he teaches the meek his ways" (Ps 25:9). The humble are those whose poor-in-spirit frame of reference exposes the shallowness of a justice rooted in the good life patterns of living that this world declares to be the purpose of life. The humble are those who are led by God to a righteousness whose substance is the sharing of God's identity with its transforming power on human identity. Humility does not lower humanity. Humility elevates humanity so that its fullness of creaturehood, empty of this world's claims of sovereignty, may bear the fruit of God's creatorship. That's a truth worth the lowliness of this world's estimation. It is the "highness" of humility's worth.

There are many rooms in humility's mansion for the lowly. And there are many rooms for the lowly in spirit who respond to God with the stewardship of their earthly possessions, which makes them companions of the poor. This is the companionship that enables them to share in the image and likeness of God's creatorship. As companions of the poor, stewards of God's goods share what they have with those who have nothing but the dignity of God-likeness, shared by both rich and poor. God dwells in the mansion of the humble, and Advent invites us to come to this house of God, where "The Lord will make his glorious voice heard" (Isa 30:30). Nothing is more paramount in this house than companionship with God and the lowly. This is the companionship we were created to enjoy. It is our justice and our righteousness. It is in this perspective that we live. It is from this perspective that we labor for those who bear the marks of this world's indictment of lowliness. To share companionship with those so indicted is to share companionship with her highness, humility.

QUESTIONS FOR YOUR REFLECTION

1. What would be your response to the contention that poor self-esteem is the sign of healthy humility?

2. It is clear from the Scriptures that all of God's creatures are good (see Gen 1:1-31). At what point does the possession of God's goods become an evil in the way of God's plan for human existence?

3. How does stewardship keep open the way of humility for those who have a sufficiency of God's created goods?

WEDNESDAY OF THE THIRD WEEK

Guns, Guts, and God. Really?

WORD

> "Woe to those who go down to Egypt for help,
>   who depend upon horses;
> Who put their trust in chariots because of their number,
>   and in horsemen because of their combined power,
> But look not to the Holy One of Israel
>   nor seek the LORD!" (Isa 31:1)

REFLECTION

The substance of hope as virtue is not perceivable to our bodily senses. The capacity of the senses to be tools of faith communication is curtailed by the functions they were created to do here on earth. To place our hope only in the substance of sense experience reduces to ignobility the identity humanity was created to be.

Isaiah's call to beware of a trust in the combined power of Egypt's military strength rather than "the Holy One of Israel" never ceases to be the prophetic call and mission of the Church. In our own day, for example, the prophetic substance of Isaiah's admonition and hope was sounded again by the pastoral letter of the U. S. Catholic bishops:

> As bishops and pastors ministering in one of the major nuclear nations, we have encountered [its] terror in the minds and hearts of our people—indeed we share it. . . . From the resources of faith we wish to provide hope and strength to all who see a world free of the nuclear threat. Hope sustains one's capacity to live with danger without being overwhelmed by it; hope is the will to struggle against obstacles even when they appear insuperable. Ultimately our hope rests in God who gave us life, sustains the world by his power, and has called us to revere the lives of every person and all peoples.[29]

The bishops call us to a hope far more substantial than the "hopes" of government leaders who insist that the stockpiling of nuclear weapons is the nation's assurance and certainty of peace. Our episcopal, prophetic voice, like Isaiah's, exposes the shallowness of "Guns, Guts, and God" as hope for security and peacemaking.

A certainty of peacemaking that counts on military prowess does not bear the fruit that is born from the resourcefulness of humanity's graced efforts to make peace. I offer three reasons why hope in this world's prowess is both problematical and futile.

First, whatever cannot survive this world cannot offer the peace that stills personhood's inner longing for survival. We mock God when we claim allegiance to God's promise of protection but trust first the promise of a nation's defenses by destruction. How interesting that the slogan of false patriotism, "Guns, Guts, and God," gives God third place. One ought to ask, which one outlasts the others?

A second reason to beware of this world's nuclear "hope" for peace lies within weaponry's primary purpose for existence. Weapons exist for destruction. The annihilation they can wreak wins not peace but fear. Fear may suspend war, but it is a suspension that can't bring peace because it can't expel fear.

Finally, we cannot be at peace when "Guns and Guts" are placed before God as a nation's boast. Those who rely on instruments of destruction as peacemakers give evidence of their mistrust in personhood's peacemakers: dialogue, diplomacy, and discernment. But above all, the protagonists of "Guns and Guts" give clear evidence of the shallow conviction that this world and its values are ultimate aims. This is the "hope" that allows any means to justify any "ideal."

Hope based on this world's ultimacy betrays shocking evidence of ignorance about human purpose. Never to hope in a transcendent reality is to stand condemned to the agony of never-to-be-quenched thirstings for a human purpose this world cannot even surmise. The quenched thirst of human purpose's longings is possible when we exercise our capacity to listen to and ponder over God's Word. We live *in,* not *of,* this world. To be in a reality but not of it is to keep ourselves open for the being we were created to become.

The voice of Advent proclaims a certainty of human purpose not rooted in this world. Advent reminds us that human purpose is of God's making. "There is one God who by his word and wisdom created all things and set them in order. His Word is our Lord Jesus Christ, who in this last age became man among men to unite end and beginning, that is, mankind and God" (St. Irenaeus, bishop).[30]

Advent is about a hope already come. As truly as Mary carried God's Word within her womb, so we bear within the mystery of our lives the hope that quenches the thirsts this world cannot. We, too, bear the indelible imprint of Jesus Christ, whose presence among us revealed humankind's purpose. Jesus, who is God in the flesh of humanity, verified that humanity was created to be in the spirit of God's divinity. To count on the substance of that certainty is the essence of hope and the reason for human nobility.

QUESTIONS FOR YOUR REFLECTION

1. In terms of her virginity, how is Mary a sacrament of the hope whose certainty lies beyond this world's capacity to promise?

2. We believe that Jesus is the Son of God. How, in the light of our belief, is the birth of Jesus indisputable evidence that God keeps his word? How is Christ's birth a sacrament and the substance of hope?

3. The purpose of human existence is humankind's creation to be the likeness of God. How does this fundamental purpose of human existence make certain our decision to trust God over "Guns and Guts"?

4. If Christ has already come into our lives, is it inconsistent for hope to be Advent's chief virtue? How do we hope for a coming that has already come? Is it inconsistent to pray "Thy kingdom come, thy will be done" and then believe that "the reign of God is already in your midst" (Luke 17:21)?

"The Innermost Things of God": Crooked Lines?

WORD

"He sent his Son, the eternal Word, who enlightens all men, to dwell among men and make known to them the innermost things of God. Jesus, the Word made flesh . . . brings to perfection the saving work that the Father gave him to do" (Constitution on Divine Revelation).[31]

REFLECTION

Someone observed, "God writes straight with crooked lines." The "innermost things of God" that Jesus revealed to be the straight line between God and humankind appeared to be crooked lines to those whose "straight line" to God linked law and humankind. Many who heard Jesus speak rebuffed his lines of thought because they considered them injurious to the Law. They looked askance at Jesus' mingling with sinners; they rejected his compassion for the poor; they repudiated his care for the mentally and physically impaired. The voice of Jesus, crying out in the desert (see Isa 40:3) of perceived unorthodoxy, became a threat to their "straight line" legalism to God.

61

Before Jesus spoke his "crooked lines," God called the Virgin Mary to become the virginal mother of Jesus. From the moment of her consent, Mary's virginal motherhood has also become a crooked line for those who have failed to discern the innermost thoughts of God. The Feast of the Immaculate Conception, a shining star in the season of Advent, invites us to ponder God's straight-line vision which includes Mary's virginal motherhood, whose "crooked line" ambiguity has perplexed the thoughts of God's people. Mary is the sign of God's voice crying out to us:

> Prepare the way of the Lord,
> make straight his paths (Matt 3:3).

The placing of Mary's immaculate conception in the season of Advent was not happenstance. Advent heralds the coming of God's Son who came to "make known . . . the innermost things of God." The mystery of Mary's immaculate conception, her total sinlessness, beckons us to follow Advent's call to enter even deeper into the innermost regions of this mystery's meaning. It is in this sanctuary of God's straight lines that the virginal motherhood of Mary calls us.

Mary's sinlessness invites us to ask, why was Mary sinless from the moment of her conception? What singular gift did God bestow upon her to make possible the gift of sinlessness? Let Mary answer the question with her own words: "Let it be done to me as you say" (Luke 1:38). God's priceless gift to Mary, the gift that made straight her way to sinlessness, was unyielding fidelity to the will of God.

Long before the angel called Mary to the motherhood of Jesus, Mary witnessed fidelity to the vow of virginity. Faithfulness to virginity's vow was not a crooked line for Mary. Rather, vowed virginity was the frame of reference in which she accepted the motherhood of Jesus. Mary did not discard her vow when she was asked to become the mother of Jesus. To the contrary, she offered her virginity as God's *straight way* to humankind through her virginal motherhood.

Mary's question, "How can this be since I do not know man?" was not one of hesitancy, doubt, or reluctance. Her question came from a profound belief that God's will for her motherhood would be done within the context of her virginity. She looked for *direction,* not combat. She asked for light that she might embrace the motherhood of Jesus within her virginal life vowed to God. Her fidelity to virginity signified her fidelity to God's will for human dignity.

Mary's fidelity to God's will evoked from God a straight-line answer that brought together the "crooked lines" of motherhood and virginity. "The Holy Spirit will come upon you and the power of the Most High will overshadow you; hence the holy offspring to be born will be called Son of God" (Luke 1:35). Mary's fidelity to virginity as the companion to her motherhood revealed her sinlessness. Mary was sinless because she had been granted faithfulness to human dignity. She had vowed virginity so that faithfulness to God, her image and likeness, might stand as the irrevocable vocation of all. The fruit of God's gift of fidelity was her life of sinlessness.

Is Mary's immaculate conception but another "crooked line," too much for us to accept? Not if faith is the ground upon which we stand. Our sinfulness from conception does not prevent subsequent fidelity to the will of God. Why? Because we have been reowned by the Son of Mary. God calls us to be faithful to our graced human dignity by remembering the purpose for which we exist. All purposes less than the God-likeness we were created to become are but crooked lines in the innermost thoughts of God. The lesser purposes of our lives become crooked lines only when we declare them to be ultimate. When we are faithful to God's purpose for human creation, we can accept the believability of Mary's marriage of virginity and motherhood.

It seems to me that sin is the refusal to let faith reveal God's innermost meanings beyond their crooked-line earthbound meanings. Faith concedes that God sees beyond the crooked lines of human comprehension. Mary was sinless because she was granted the gift of fidelity to human purpose. She believed that God created her for a destiny beyond this world's specifications for happiness. Her fidelity to human dignity protected her from Eve's sin of allegiance to the lesser gods of this world.

"God writes straight with crooked lines!" Isaiah agrees:

> . . . the spirit from on high
>   is poured out on us.
> Then will the desert become an orchard
>   and the orchard be regarded as a forest.
> Right will dwell in the desert
>   and justice abide in the orchard.
> Justice will bring about peace;
>   right will produce calm and security (Isa 32:15-17).

QUESTIONS FOR YOUR REFLECTION

1. Recall crooked lines in your life. Have you been able to see these lines become straight lines? Have you been able to see the hand of God as he wrote straight the lines of your life?

2. Will negative attitudes toward unanswered prayer change if we understand prayer as the straight line into God's innermost mind?

3. Is the question, how can this be possible evidence of pride? In what way, however, did Mary's use of that question reveal her faith and humility?

4. Is Mary's virginal motherhood of Jesus, within the context of her vow to remain virginal, significant to those who are tempted to regard vowed chastity and celibacy as "crooked lines" in religious life and holy orders?

FRIDAY OF THE THIRD WEEK

Prayer Is Unceasing Longing for God

WORD

"The desire of your heart is itself your prayer. And if your desire is constant, so is your prayer. The apostle Paul had a purpose in saying: 'Pray without ceasing' (1 Thess 5:17). Are we then ceaselessly to bend on our knees, to be prostrate, or to lift up our hands? Is this what is meant in saying: 'Pray without ceasing'?

"There is another, interior kind of prayer without ceasing, namely, the desire of the heart. . . . If you wish to pray without ceasing, do not cease to desire" (St. Augustine, bishop).[32]

REFLECTION

After St. Paul's comment to the Romans, "We ourselves, although we have the Spirit as first fruits, groan inwardly," he adds: "The Spirit

. . . makes intercession for us with groanings that cannot be expressed in speech" (Rom 8:23, 26). To be noticed in this comment is the sharing of groanings between God and the human person. These mutual and ceaseless groanings by God and humanity arise from our longings to achieve God's created purpose for humankind. God's Spirit joins our spirit in the longing to see humanity fully sharing God's identity.

St. Augustine proposes that the ceaseless desires of God and humankind are what St. Paul means by ceaseless prayer: "The constancy of your desire," St. Augustine writes, "will itself be the ceaseless voice of your prayer."[33] Here St. Paul and St. Augustine bridge four centuries to confirm the good news that the agony of the anguished longings of God and humanity is at the heart of genuine and unceasing prayer. It is genuine because it gives rise to our desire for God; it is unceasing because, except for despair, that desire will never die until we are fully one with God for all eternity.

There is no doubt that the basis of our longing for God is the unfulfilled intimacy with God we were created to enjoy forever. Our earthly lives do not fully possess that intimacy. We groan unceasingly, often without knowing why, for a purpose carved into our being. Not to enjoy the fullness of that purpose here upon earth is why we groan with St. Augustine, "For you have made us for yourself, and our heart is restless until it rests in you."[34]

Longings to share full intimacy with God are at the heart of many unfulfilled or broken intimacies: longings of parents who desire to hold again their deceased children; longings of children whose divorced parents once gave them the intimacy of family life—their childhood's environment of belonging; longings of addicts who groan inwardly for the transcendence they once traded for the highs of chemical dependency; longings of victims of terminal illness who groan with anguish for the gift of extended life on earth; longings of those whose ceaseless sufferings find them yearning to leave this world for an eternity with God.

These longings are ceaseless because God's groanings for intimacy with us will never cease. The groanings of both God and humankind spring from a profound not-of-this-world longing for intimacy, belonging, and communion. The three Persons of God's identity are one, and it is this intimacy of perfect wholeness we were created to embody and become.

Deep longings determine one's final thoughts as death approaches.

In his last discourse to the disciples, Jesus voiced the deepest longing of his life here upon earth:

> I pray that they may be [one] in us,
> that the world may believe that you sent me.
> I have given them the glory you gave me
> that they may be one as we are one—
> I living in them, you living in me—
> that their unity may be complete (John 17:21-23).

Here Jesus lets us into the innermost realm of God's life that we might see why God groans in the innermost realm of our life. God's deepest longing is to share with us the fullness of communion that can only be found in God's trinitarian life. God's longing that we share in that communion is also our longing to share a life of intimacy, belonging, and communion with God.

The mutual groanings of God and humankind is really the essence of prayer. It is the prayer that speaks love and makes vivid the solidarity we have with God and with one another, even when we cannot express that solidarity with words. The grief of separation here on earth never leaves us. The presence of grief, however, offers us the joy and peace of knowing that its presence is the heartbeat of God's unceasing prayerful longing for mutual identity with humankind.

The voice of Advent's prophet, Isaiah, cries out this joyful news in the midst of Israel's darkest hour:

> To the people of alien tongue you will look no more,
> the people of obscure speech,
> stammering in a language not understood.
> Look to Zion, the city of our festivals;
> let your eyes see Jerusalem
> as a quiet abode, a tent not to be struck,
> Whose pegs will never be pulled up,
> nor its ropes severed. . . .
> No one who dwells there will say, "I am sick" (Isa 33:19-20, 24).

QUESTIONS FOR YOUR REFLECTION

1. Is it possible that groaning, once regarded as agony, might become a source of consolation and peace? How?

2. Our own deepest groanings are the heartbeats of God's longing heart. God longs to be one with us. What is the relationship between that

longing and Christ's words "How blest are the poor in spirit" (Matt 5:3)?

3. Read the story of the prodigal son (see Luke 15:11-24). What does the image of the father say about God's longing for us?

4. How are groanings and longings within us a sign of God's presence? Can you explain why the groanings and longings of God and humankind are unceasing prayer?

There Are No More "Outsiders"!

WORD

"Thus says the LORD,
    the Holy One of Israel, his maker:
You question me about my children,
    or prescribe the work of my hands for me!
It was I who made the earth
    and created mankind upon it;
It was my hands that stretched out the heavens;
    I gave the order to all their host.
It was I who stirred up one for the triumph of justice;
    all his ways I make level.
He shall rebuild my city
    and let my exiles go free
Without price or ransom,
    says the LORD of hosts" (Isa 45:11-13).

REFLECTION

No human being stands outside God's purpose. That purpose is justice and peace for all human beings, either as recipients of purpose's gift or as instruments of its achievement.

Though he was not of God's chosen people, Cyrus II, "shepherd" of the Persian Empire, was a fruitful instrument in the restoration of justice and peace for God's people. Formerly an ally of Babylon, Cyrus broke away from that alliance in 593 B.C. and liberated thousands of Israelites whom the Babylonians had carried away into captivity.

The work of Cyrus did not go unnoticed. Speaking for God, Isaiah cries out:

> I say of Cyrus: My shepherd,
>   who fulfills my every wish;
> He shall say of Jerusalem "Let her be rebuilt."
>   and of the temple, "Let its foundations be laid. . . ."
> I have called you by your name,
>   giving you a title, though you knew me not. . . .
> It was I who stirred up one for the triumph of justice; . . .
>   (Isa 44:28; 45:4, 13).

Each year Advent brings before us the name of Cyrus to remind us that in the sight of God there are no "outsiders," banned from being instruments of Christ's coming. Advent asks, is God's work an "inside job," to be carried out only by a special lineage carefully groomed by God? If St. Matthew's lineage of Christ (see Matt 1:1-17) were the only one available, we might be hard put to argue for a broader lineage of Christ's coming. Happily, St. Luke makes available a broader list of Jesus' ancestors (see Luke 3:23-38). Unlike Matthew's Gospel, Luke's Gospel traces the lineage of Jesus from Joseph to Adam rather than from Mary to Abraham. Within Luke's vast scope of ancestors, there are included representatives from all of humanity. There are no "outsiders"—all of humanity qualifies for the lineage of Jesus.

St. Leo the Great touches on this:

> Unless the new man, by being made in the likeness of sinful humanity, had taken on himself the nature of our first parents, unless he had stooped to be one in substance with his mother while sharing the Father's substance and, being alone free from sin, united our nature to his, the whole human race would still be held captive under the dominion of Satan.[35]

There are no "outsiders" in St. Luke's lineage of Jesus because all were created in the image and likeness of God. Christ's lineage was not the exclusive property of those whose lives were formed and shaped by the Law that defined God's "insiders." God sent Jesus Christ to be the universal definition of humanity's purpose. Jesus came from a lineage of sinful humanity that the sinfulness of human nature might be put to death. Jesus also came from the sinless humanity of Mary that from her virginity Jesus might be revealed as the Son of God the Father.

Jesus spent a great deal of his time with the "outsiders," whose physical, mental, and spiritual poverties placed them outside the Law's credentials for salvation. The Law branded them sinners, saying that their poverties deprived them of belonging to God and humankind. Not so with Jesus. He was fond of these "sinners" not because of their sins (see John 8:11) but because his vision of humanity's belonging extended far beyond that of the Jewish magisterium. In his mind the "sinners," so declared by a Law that placed them outside salvation's belonging, were justified by the created purpose God designed for all of humanity.

Jesus became an "outsider" himself. Why? Because he taught that authentic insiders were those who lived according to a fundamental belonging rooted in God's identity. Jesus insisted that all human beings belong to God by way of creation and grace, not law. He taught that humankind's authentic belonging also extended horizontally to include the created solidarity all men and women have in common. This is what Jesus meant when he said:

> " 'You shall love the Lord your God
> with your whole heart,
> with your whole soul,
> and with all your mind.'
>
> This is the greatest and first commandment. The second is like it;
>
> 'You shall love your neighbor as yourself' " (Matt 22:37-38, NAB, 1970).

Here, Jesus defined his lineage. He considered no one outside the parameters of love because *God is love.* No one was outside that love, not even Cyrus, "shepherd" of the Persian Empire and God's "anointed" one (see Isa 45:1) nor, for that matter, the good thief who from the cross cried out for communion with Jesus in his kingdom. Little wonder that the spirit of Advent joyfully proclaims: There are no more "outsiders"!

QUESTIONS FOR YOUR REFLECTION

1. How does St. Matthew's lineage of Jesus differ from St. Luke's? If you had written your version of the gospel solely for a Jewish readership, which of the two Gospel lineages would you have chosen? Simi-

larly, if your readership had been primarily Gentiles, which lineage would have been your choice?

2. We live in the twentieth century. In what sense do we share in the lineage of Jesus? Does the sacrament of baptism call for a responsibility to hand on to unborn generations our witness of Christ's presence to us? Does this handing on suggest a yet-to-be-born presence of Christ?

3. In what sense was Jesus' human presence a yet-to-be-born presence? What is the Church's sacramental and advent role in that unborn presence of Christ?

4. In what way was Cyrus an outsider in the eyes of the Jews and an insider in the eyes of God? Don't we sometimes play the insider-outsider game when we engage in racism, denominationalism, sexism, and nationalism?

DECEMBER 18

See God? Look with the Eyes of Faith

WORD

"No man has ever seen God or known him, but God has revealed himself to us through faith, by which it is possible to see him" (Letter to Diognetus).[36]

REFLECTION

A young man visited an old monk renowned for his prayerfulness. "Father," pleaded the exuberant lad, "teach me to pray."

Saying nothing, the monk summoned the eager neophyte to follow him down the road. Intrigued, the youth reflected, "This holy man is reminding me that the road to holiness is a journey and I must pray as I go."

In time, they arrived at the shore of a river where the hermit led his excited follower out to its deepest point. Again, the young man raised his thoughts to lofty heights: "Oh, how mystical," he prayed, "he's reminding me of my baptism."

Suddenly the monk grasped the young man's head and plunged him beneath the water. Again, the aspirant's mind soared to the heavens of contemplation. "Now I see!" he exlaimed. "He is teaching me that to pray I must first renounce all of my sinfulness."

The monk showed no signs of releasing his grip and soon the youth grew apprehensive. As time passed, apprehension turned to desperation and the terrified young man began to struggle violently to free himself from the monk's viselike grip. At the last moment he wrenched himself away and emerged from the water, gasping for air.

When he was able to regain his speech, the thoroughly disillusioned youth angrily shouted, "What's the matter with you, old man? I asked you to teach me how to pray and you tried to drown me!"

The monk broke his silence and said quietly, "Sir, when you want to pray as desperately to the God you are yet to know as you violently wanted to survive the God you thought you knew, come back and see me."[37]

The old monk is symbolic of God, while the young man represents any of us whose faith extends no further than the expectations *we* have of the God we imagine. The story is about prayer, but especially about prayer in faith to the divine being the monk believed to be incomprehensible and unimaginable. This is not to say that our images of God are worthless. They have worth and value as long as they grow, develop, and call us in faith to the identity of God's incomprehensibility. Images of God are worthless, however, when they become our determinants of God's identity. When that happens, who needs faith?

Are we really practicing authentic faith when we expect our fixed images of God to be God's definition? When expectations of God fit definitions of God, we run the risk of prayerfulness to a deity we understand rather than believe. The God we can understand is the one we have created in our image and likeness.

What we imagine to be a test of faith may be only a test of what we expect of our easy-to-understand image of God. On one occasion, Jesus tested his disciples' expectations of their image of his messiahship. Endeavoring to dispel their terror as they saw him walk the stormy waters of the lake, he said calmly, "It is I. Do not be afraid!" (Matt 14:27) Peter cried out, "Lord, if it is really you, tell me to come to you across the water" (Matt 14:28). Peter sank beneath the water because he went for a faith that took him out of the boat rather than the faith he could have shown without his ever having left the boat.

Sometimes God lets us come to him by way of our own expectations so that we might watch them sink beneath the waters of our faith in them. Like the old monk, God allows us to follow him in terms of our expectations so that when they are submerged we can at least suspect that God is more than our expectations will allow. "No man has ever seen God or known him, but God has revealed himself to us through faith."

To expect God to be God within the parameters of expectations rooted in a fixed human image of divinity is to remove faith's capacity to make possible a vision of God that no apparition can provide. Faith enlightens and strengthens reasoning's capacity to see that God is. Faith is full strength not because it can reveal what God sees but because it can reveal the certainty that God sees a destiny for us we simply can't imagine. Full-strength faith moves us to cry out, "Lord, show us your kindness" (see Ps 85:8), even when there is not the faintest clue what form that kindness will take.

Faith is not genuine when we insist on seeing God in terms of our capacity to see this world's display of the spectacular. God asked through Isaiah:

> Whom would you compare me with, as an equal,
> or match me against, as though we were alike (Isa 46:5)?

Faith fails when we expect it to reveal God in apparitions of heaven garmented with our images of power and beauty. Faith is much quieter than its imagined capacity to help us walk on water. God's presence needs only the whisper of faith not because God can't be compared to this world's marvels but because God does not need the accompaniment of the noise they often create. The old monk had nothing to offer the young man except the opportunity to decide whether he really had a desire to pray to the God who is clothed with incomprehensibility. The would-be disciple desperately needed to rid his heart of expectations whose noise drowned out the whispers of genuine faith.

This is the faith that Advent offers us. It proclaims that Christ does not live in some disembodied existence apart from this world's realities. True faith challenges us to see Christ not in the coming of an apparition of Christ, whom we have garmented with the triumphalism of our expectations, but in the coming of Christ, whose quiet, ecclesial presence is with the poor. The Church is the body of Christ commissioned for compassion among the poor. We are the Church, and we bear the responsibility of standing with those whose only remaining power is to whisper a cry for help. That is why Christ entrusts himself to our faith in the Eucharist's real presence, so that the poor might hear him quietly speak through our real presence, "It is I, do not be afraid."

QUESTIONS FOR YOUR REFLECTION

1. Why is faith necessary at the point where understanding cannot cope?

2. In the story of the monk and the young man, what weakness in the young man posed itself as a masquerade of faith when he followed the old monk to the water?

3. Does a reluctance to abide by external changes in the Church indicate that perhaps there has not been a change in one's image of God or Church? Why is an unchanged image of God from childhood days perhaps a suggestion that one is risking idolatry?

4. Is it contradictory to say that God can't be seen, yet God can be seen? What is it of God that can't be seen? What is it of God that can be seen?

DECEMBER 19

What Shape Are We in?

WORD

> *"If man, without being puffed up or boastful, has a right belief regarding created things and their Creator, who, having given them being, holds them all in his power, and if man perseveres in God's love, and in obedience and gratitude to him, he will receive greater glory from him. It will be a glory which will grow ever brighter until he takes on the likeness of the one who died for him"* (St. Irenaeus, bishop).[38]

73

REFLECTION

St. Irenaeus offers us four evidences that God is active within us, forming and shaping us in "the likeness of the one who died. . . ." These evidences are "a right belief regarding created things and their Creator," perseverence in God's love, obedience, and gratitude.

St. Irenaeus is not offering us ways we might qualify for the image and likeness of God. He offers us ways we might long for total surrender to "the likeness of the one who died for [us]," a likeness we already possess. These four ways of re-forming our lives around the centrality of God-likeness enable "a glory which will grow ever brighter." There are evidences that this glory is active in our lives.

The first evidence is enthronement of God's sovereignty at the center of our lives:

> I will yield to no entreaty,
> says our redeemer,
> Whose name is the LORD of hosts,
> the Holy One of Israel (Isa 47:3-4).

With this centering, faith, liberated from the periphery of our lives where former centerings of this world's temporalities placed it, offers us "a right belief regarding created things." God's glory is at work within us when created things are no longer at the center of our attention. Isaiah lashed out at the Babylonians for the arrogance of proclaiming themselves sovereign rulers over the whole world. Speaking in God's name, Isaiah deplored the sovereignty that the "virgin daughter" Babylon had claimed for herself:

> Come down, sit in the dust,
> O virgin daughter Babylon; . . .
> Go into darkness and sit in silence,
> O daughter of the Chaldeans,
> No longer shall you be called
> sovereign mistress of kingdoms (Isa 47:1, 5).

An unmistakable evidence that we are becoming like God is the profound reverence we hold for our *creaturehood*. We stand before God glorious when we have spent our lives pursuing the vocation of becoming intimate with God by way of our creaturely existence. This is what becoming human means. It is the vocation of emptying ourselves not of the use of this world's goods but of the false belief that their possession endows us with the powers of sovereignty.

Human development is the pursuit of creaturehood. It is not the "humanism" that sees only technology at the center of human development. Rather, human development stems from "a right belief regarding created things," whereby we find the meaning of creaturehood in the light of God's sovereign creatorship. The presence of this right belief is uncontested evidence that we are growing in the likeness of God our Creator.

St. Irenaeus next turns to persevering love as evidence of God's glory unfolding in our lives. The love of which he speaks is *agape,* a word for love seldom used among the Greeks because it was regarded as an impossible way to love.

Agape cares only for God and for others. It is deeply conscious that God, not self, is at the center of human existence. With the aid of faith's clarity, *agape* sees that human purpose is the sharing in God's way, truth, and life. It stands on the premise that "God is love" (1 John 4:16). For that reason, *agape* expects absolutely no return other than the joy of sharing with God the very likeness of God.

> God is love,
> and he who abides in love
> abides in God,
> and God in him (1 John 4:16).

Those who love in the *agape* way see their possessions as instruments of God's love and compassion and themselves as the stewards. Those who love in *agape's* way persevere because it becomes evident that God's image and likeness, "I AM," is also humankind's "I am."

A third evidence of God's inner activity within us is obedience. Authentic obedience is never a deterrent. It does not thwart us or leave us unfulfilled, nor does it prevent us from becoming human. Obedience is the key that lets us gain entrance into the unexplored realms of human mystery from whence the hiddenness of personhood's wondrous self cries out to be discovered.

To "obey" means to "listen." Those who love in the *agape* way need the Beloved's listening because this leads them into the depths of human mystery, where they find what *agape* sees—the likeness of God. Obedience puts us in touch with the indescribable fruits of that discovery: peace and joy.

Not long before he died, Thomas Merton wrote in a burst of joy, "I feel as if my whole being were an act of thanksgiving."[39] Merton's observation about himself verifies the presence of St. Irenaeus' fourth evidence of God's glory active within us. Thanksgiving is not so much a human response for God's gifts as it is the felt experience of God's inner presence.

Thanksgiving of one's whole being is God's inner testimony that there is no reason for existence other than as creaturehood's earthly dwelling place for God's kingdom. Thanksgiving is not some*thing* we do to "get" God's kingdom. Thanksgiving is the presence of God's kingdom, proclaiming our identities as its dwelling place at the center of our lives.

A right belief about creaturehood, *agape*, obedience, and thanksgiving are evidences that God's glory is active within us. Does Advent have better news?

QUESTIONS FOR YOUR REFLECTION

1. If God's image is creatorship, how do we become the image and likeness of God by pursuing creaturehood?

2. How would you explain what St. Irenaeus calls the "right belief regarding created things"?

3. If God is truly at the center of our lives, then, in the light of *agape's* meaning, are we consistent when our attitude toward created possessions is expressed "*my* possessions"?

4. What is the difference between obedience and subservience?

5. Why is thanksgiving a beautiful summary of St. Irenaeus' four evidences of God's active meaning for our human purpose?

Must We Weary God with Our Possibles?

WORD

"From now on I announce new things to you,
hidden events of which you knew not.
Now, not long ago, they are brought into being,
and beforetime you did not hear of them,
so that you cannot claim to have known them;
You neither heard nor knew,
they did not reach your ears beforehand.
Yes, I know you are utterly treacherous,
a rebel you were called from birth" (Isa 48:6-8).

REFLECTION

To ask of God answers and solutions that meet the requirements of our reasoning and imagination is to weary God with our possibles. To seek from God only the understandable is to have a god much too small for human creaturehood's graced capacity to believe.

Our creaturehood is like God not in terms of equality with God but in terms of our unlimited capacity to believe that God can do the impossible, the unimaginable, and the incomprehensible. God longs to be touched, and faith makes touching God a reality. Faith accepts the truth that there are no limits to the possibilities of God's love. It proclaims that while God is infinitely more than our creaturehood can imagine, our capacity to believe is also infinitely more than our creaturehood can surmise. We possess a faith that enables us to be in touch with God's unimaginable love.

We weary God when we allow God's creatorship no more room than imagination can provide. "Weary" is not my word; it is the word God used in response to Ahaz, king of Judah, who refused to ask God for the unimaginable: "The LORD spoke to Ahaz: Ask for a sign from the LORD, your God; let it be deep as the nether world, or high as the sky! But Ahaz answered, 'I will not ask! I will not tempt the Lord!' Then [the Lord] said: Listen, O house of David! Is it not enough for you to weary men, must you also weary my God!" (Isa 7:10-13)

What wearies God is a faithlessness that refuses to let God be God. It is a faithlessness that prevents God from being Creator. It is a faithlessness that, while acknowledging that God created the world, demands that creatorship be limited to boundaries our imaginations have already created. What is so wearying about this faithlessness is its denial of humanity's graced capacity to believe as "deep as the nether world, or [as] high as the sky!"

God's creatorship continues to create precisely where, in our imagination, there is only "a formless wasteland" (Gen 1:2). Here in the wasteland of Ahaz's faithlessness God responded with "therefore," the preface to divine "logic." "Therefore the LORD himself will give you this sign: the virgin shall be with child, and bear a son, and shall name him Immanuel" (Isa 7:14).

The weakness of Ahaz paved the way for the "logic" that moved God to reveal a reality adequate for faith but heretofore foreign to human imagination. God's "therefore" prefaced the sign of God's boundless creatorship and creaturehood's limitless, graced capacity to touch God through faith. God's inaccessibility became touchable because God is *Immanuel,* that is, "God is with us."

In a book of splendid Advent essays, Fr. Raymond E. Brown writes:

> Zechariah and Elizabeth in their piety have been yearning for a child . . . but Mary is a virgin who has not been intimate with her husband, so that what happens is not a response to her yearning but a surprise initiative by God that neither Mary nor Joseph could have anticipated. The Baptist's conception, while a gift of God, involved an act of human intercourse. Mary's conception involves a divine creative action without human intercourse; it is the work of the overshadowing Spirit, that same Spirit that hovered at the creation of the world when all was void.[40]

Advent calls us to a pilgrimage of faith ready to carry us beyond the horizons of what we can imagine and understand. St. Bernard's plea to Mary is Advent's plea to us:

> Open your heart to faith, O Blessed Virgin, your lips to praise, your womb to the Creator. See, the desired of all nations is at your door, knocking to enter. If he should pass by because of your delay, in sorrow you would begin to seek him afresh, the One whom your soul loves. Arise, hasten, open. Arise in faith, hasten in devotion,

open in praise and thanksgiving. "Behold the handmaid of the Lord," she says, "be it done to me according to your word" (Luke 1:38).[41]

QUESTIONS FOR YOUR REFLECTION

1. Does not God's gift of virginal motherhood through which Mary put us in touch with Jesus also suggest a similarity to God's gift of faith and its capacity to put us in touch with God? How would you explain the similarity?
2. What is it that above all wearies God?
3. Keeping God within the boundaries of our imagination is the futility of creating God in our image and likeness. How can faith prevent us from that futility?
4. To what are you opening yourself when you "open your heart to faith"?

DECEMBER 21

Beyond Imagination Lies the Journey of Faith

WORD

> *"You also are blessed because you have heard and believed. A soul that believes both conceives and brings forth the Word of God and acknowledges his works.*
> *"Let Mary's soul be in each of you to proclaim the greatness of the Lord. Let her spirit be in each of you to rejoice in the Lord. Christ has only one mother in the flesh, but we all bring forth Christ in faith"* (St. Ambrose, bishop).[42]

REFLECTION

If God is more than we can humanly imagine, faith enables us to reap a fruitfulness likewise humanly unimaginable. The seeds of faith

79

we sow will reap fruits we can hardly imagine but which we can warmly receive.

Mary's visit to her cousin Elizabeth tells of a fruitfulness far beyond imagination. God's Word spoke from Mary's womb to the womb of Elizabeth, and the unimaginable happened. "When Elizabeth heard Mary's greeting, the baby leapt in her womb [and] Elizabeth . . . was filled with the Holy Spirit and cried out in a loud voice: 'Blest are you among women and blest is the fruit of your womb'" (Luke 1:41-42).

Mary's words to Elizabeth enabled the Word of her womb to speak his grace to John the Baptist. When Elizabeth heard Mary's words, the leap of her unborn proclaimed for all generations the joy of his wombed cleansing. Our imagination yields to faith when the story of Mary's visitation is told. Yet our gift of faith, the same faith with which Mary welcomed God's Word into her virginal womb, enables us to welcome the coming of the Word of God into our lives. Mary trusted God precisely at the point where the fruit of her virginal womb, Jesus, defied imagination.

This is the trust that Advent invites us to embrace, so that our hearts may leap with joy as we acknowledge God's continuous coming. Advent calls us to trust that which we can't imagine and to count on a fruitfulness of joy impossible to describe.

It is not required of us that we fully analyze Advent's fruitfulness. God asks only that we proclaim in faith and with joy the "great things" God has done for us. St. Ambrose comments: "Let Mary's soul be in each of you to proclaim the greatness of the Lord. Let her spirit be in each to rejoice in the Lord."[43] Indeed, Mary found it impossible to describe the fruit of her womb and the joy of Jesus' presence. She could only exclaim:

> My being proclaims the greatness of the Lord,
>   my spirit finds joy in God my savior,
> For he has looked upon his servant in her lowliness;
>   all ages to come shall call me blessed.
> God who is mighty has done great things for me,
>   holy is his name. . . (Luke 1:46-49).

Why does joylessness sometimes bespeak our relationship with God? Might it not be that we won't let God be God? To let God be God is to possess the poverty of spirit that awaits and expects a fruitfulness without even a hint of who we imagine God to be. A relationship with God becomes joyless when we approach God with expectations solely ours. Joyless Christians tend to ask God only for that which they *expect* God to grant, good as those expectations may be. Joyless Christians, alas, plot and chart God. They want God to be in their image and likeness, bearing a fruitfulness likewise their image and likeness. They are joyless because their God is well within their imaginations. That makes God too small for them. 'Tis a pity!

A God too small for the purpose of human creation is why Isaiah pleaded:

> Listen to me, Jacob,
>> Israel whom I named!
> I, it is I who am first,
>> and also the last am I.
> Yes, my hand laid the foundations of the earth;
>> my right hand spread out my heavens.
> When I call them,
>> they stand forth at once. . . .
>> Who among you foretold these things?
> The LORD's friend shall do his will
>> against Babylon and the progeny of Chaldea (Isa 48:12-14).

How significant that Isaiah wrote, "The Lord's friend shall do his will against Babylon and the progeny of Chaldea." How unimaginable! Was there a person chosen by God to bring down the prowess of Babylon and Chaldea? There was. It was of this "friend" that God spoke, again through Isaiah:

> I say of Cyrus: My shepherd,
>> who fulfills my every wish;
> He shall say of Jerusalem, "Let her be rebuilt . . ." (Isa 44:28).

Suggested in the story of Mary's visitation is an important Advent credential for God's friendship. The Lord asks only for our human presence, through which God longs to be "magnified." St. Ambrose notes:

> The Lord is magnified, not because the human voice can add anything to God but because he is magnified within us. Christ is the image of God, and if the soul does what is right and holy, it magnifies the image of God in whose likeness it was created and, in magnifying the image of God, the soul has a share in its greatness and is exalted.[44]

God does not require that we analyze divine presence within us. We are asked only to proclaim what God has done for us, through us, with us, and in us. To let God be God at the point where both imagination and analysis fail is to be a "friend" of God, never ceasing to leap for joy in the womb of faith.

QUESTIONS FOR YOUR REFLECTION

1. St. Ambrose says that we are blessed if we hear and believe. What is the connection between hearing God's word and believing God's Word? What is the difference between hearing with your ears and listening with your heart?

2. While imagination cannot keep pace with God's transcendence, it can grow and develop when we exercise God's gift of faith. Can you recall times when acts of true faith later enabled your imagination to expand?

3. The fruits of the Holy Spirit are "love, joy, peace, patient endurance, kindness, generosity, faith, mildness, and chastity" (Gal 5:22-23). Have you experienced at least one of these? If so, is it significant that your imagination cannot describe the experience? How did Mary verbally respond to her experience of the Holy Spirit's fruitfulness in her womb (see Luke 1:46-55) when she visited her cousin Elizabeth?

4. In what respect is the visitation story an important feature of Advent's meaning?

5. Does the mystery of Mary's visitation support the Church's claim to be, by nature, apostolic and mission minded?

"Even Should She Forget . . ."

WORD

"Can a mother forget her infant,
be without tenderness for the child of her womb?
Even should she forget,
I will never forget you.
See, upon the palms of my hands I have written your
name; . . .
See, I will lift up my hand to the nations,
and raise my signal to the peoples" (Isa 49:15-16, 22).

REFLECTION

Circumcision was evidence of fidelity to God's covenant among God's chosen people. Its mark represented a permanent faithfulness to God's covenant not only in terms of one's personal intent but also in terms of one's determination to hand on covenanted fidelity to future generations.

Modesty and propriety kept hidden circumcision's physical mark of faithfulness to God. But evidence of one's unfaithfulness to the spirit of God's covenant could not be hidden. It was revealed by an obvious inconsistency between the imperative to be circumcised and the imperative to give witness of the circumcised's fidelity to covenant's promise of holiness.

But permanence of fidelity was not to be a one-sided matter. God did not ask the chosen people for bodily marks of their permanence of intention without first giving evidence of divinity's intention to be forever faithful to the covenant. While marks of circumcision, though permanent, very often became a mark of judgment against those unfaithful to God's covenant, nowhere could the prophets find evidence of God's unfaithfulness to love and compassion. To those who complained of God's infidelity, Isaiah asked in God's name:

Can a mother forget her infant. . . ?
Even should she forget,
I will never forget you.

In the mind of Isaiah, motherhood represented the permanence of the tenderness love carves on the hearts of all mothers. At the same time, it was conceivable to the prophet that hardness of heart might cause a mother to forget her child. Could the same also be said of God? Was it conceivable that God's fidelity to the covenant might also suffer motherhood's occasional forgetfulness? Never! "See," God spoke through Isaiah, "upon the palms of my hands I have written your name." The prophet's point? God's fidelity to humankind is as indelibly carved on divine identity as the scar of a bodily incision on physical identity.

Think of it! Our names are eternally inscribed on the very being of God. The divine hands never cease working for God's children, because all human beings are forever marked with the likeness of God's image. That is not all. Humanity was also created to *reveal* the identity of God. This is not because humanity adds something to God, but because it enables God to proclaim divinity's greatness among all men and women. St. Bede, commenting on Mary's hymn of praise, "My soul proclaims the greatness of the Lord" (Luke 1:46), writes: "The Lord has exalted me by a gift so great, so unheard of, that language is useless to describe it, and the depths of love in my heart can scarcely grasp it."[45]

Our names are carved on the palms of God's hands. We shall always be the untiring concern of God's maternal and paternal workmanship. God bears the image and likeness of both fatherhood and motherhood. We give to God our identity that God might mediate to us the divine identity all men and women were created to become. We are like God, and in Christ, God is like us. Christ's incarnation is the evidence that God has permanently carved into heaven's identity the identity of our humanity.

God's love was carved on the hands of the risen Christ. "Take your finger and examine my hands," Christ challenged the once-unbelieving Thomas. Forever marked on the hands of the risen Christ's humanity were evidences of God's eternal faithfulness to all of humanity. But those scarred hands also gave evidence of humanity's crucified identity, carved forever on God. God created humankind to be God's likeness. But it became divinely paradoxical that humanity's created purpose became divinity's redeemed purpose.

Most of us are not called to explain, describe, analyze, or define incarnation. Praise God for theologians! But we are called to proclaim the greatness of God, who has not only marked us with the identity of heaven but has also marked heaven with earth's redeemed identity.

We often miss the mark of giving evidence that we are the image and likeness of God. But it is inconceivable that the mark of our image and likeness will ever be erased from the identity of God. "See, upon the palms of my hands I have written your name."

QUESTIONS FOR YOUR REFLECTION

1. What are your thoughts about the possibility that more emphasis on God's fidelity to humanity might arouse in us a firmer trust in God?

2. Why is Isaiah's reference to the inscription of our names "upon the palms of [God's] hands" an excellent image of God's fidelity to the covenant? Cite some examples of Jesus' permanence of fidelity that he reflected in his conduct and in his teachings?

3. What is the significance of our names written on the hands of God? What is the difference between name and number as the means of identifying human beings?

4. Why were the marks of Jesus' crucifixion signs of his glory? Does the imprint of your human identity on God's identity make a difference in the way you relate to God? Does this mutuality of identities give prayer a renewal for which people have been searching?

DECEMBER 23

Earth's Joys: Garment for Heaven's

WORD

> "There is only one God. . . . God was all alone and nothing existed but himself when he determined to create the world. . . . Apart from God there was simply nothing else" (St. Hippolytus, priest).[46]

REFLECTION

Consumerism has the capacity to cut people off at their roots. Should materialism's people not even wonder who they are, from whence they have come, or why they exist, the most consumerism can offer is a life of futility.

True happiness is not possible when a consumable existence is society's sole and ultimate purpose. Why? Because the voice whose echo unceasingly reverberates from the eternal depths of humanity's Godlike purpose will not cease to disturb. This voice cares that we experience the joy God created humankind to possess for all eternity. Isaiah writes:

> Listen to me, you who pursue justice,
>   who seek the LORD;
> Look to the rock from which you were hewn,
>   to the pit from which you were quarried (Isa 51:1).

The voice of consumerism does not sound from such depths. It speaks only from the shallow surfaces of its products. Consumerism's voice is not from "the rock from which [we] were hewn" but from the perishable realities unbecoming human destiny's imperishability. This voice first spoke through the Garden of Eden's serpentine intruder, whose unceasing lie remains consumerism's parentage: "God knows well that the moment you eat of it [this world's perishability] your eyes will be opened and you will be like gods . . ." (Gen 3:5).

First addressed to humankind's parents, this lie promised them no more than to be cut away from their divine parentage. The "rock from which [they] were hewn" was the identity they already possessed from God's creation. The serpent's lie continues to market its shallow promises of imperishability this very day.

Adam and Eve were created to be measured by the image and likeness of God. "God was all alone and nothing existed but himself when he determined to create the world. . . . Apart from God there was simply nothing else." God all alone? Was there nothing relatable in God's identity whereby human identity might measure progress in becoming like God? Pope Paul VI, in his beautiful apostolic exhortation, suggests that Christian joy is God's mode of revelation whereby all men and women might measure their oneness with the one God. He writes:

> Christian joy could not be properly praised if one were to remain indifferent to the outward and inward witness that God the Creator renders to himself in the midst of his creation: "And God saw that it was good" (Gen 1:10). Raising up man in the setting of a universe that is the work of his power, wisdom and love, and even

before manifesting himself personally according to the mode of revelation, God disposes the mind and the heart of his creature to meet joy, at the same time as truth.[47]

Pope Paul VI clearly affirms the goodness of this world's creation. He contends that within the limitless realm of God's goodness is the capacity to witness heaven's joy by way of creaturely joys. Creation is the garment of heaven's joy. It is a garment that does not deserve either the consumerism with which we measure the illusion of ultimate joy or the disdain with which we condemn creation's capacity to be enjoyed. Creation is the garment by which God mediates heaven's joy "in the midst of his creation."

Advent summons us to rejoice in our human identity because it was created by God to be the garment for Christ's identity. This is the garment the Church identifies as the incarnation. The joy of Advent's season lies in the good news that heaven's joy can be touched, experienced, and enjoyed by way of creation. Yes, "there is only one God"; yes, "God was all alone and nothing existed but himself when he determined to create the world"; yes, "apart from God there was simply nothing else." Be that as it may, the God "all alone" is the God who loved us so much that he garmented the joys of heaven with the joys of creation that we might "taste and see how good the LORD is" (Ps 34:9). That's the taste creation groans to share. She longs to be God's humble vesture that we might garment ourselves with the joy of God's vesture (see Rom 8:22).

QUESTIONS FOR YOUR REFLECTION

1. Why is consumerism today's tragedy of tragedies?

2. Could you make a case for the possibility that consumerism among Christians may be a greater danger to faith than atheism?

3. In what sense could it be held that the obedience of our first parents to the serpent's lie was the original sin (see Gen 3:1-7)? Was their obedience to the serpent's lie original because it was the first sin or because it was the source sin from whence all sins arise?

4. St. Paul writes, "We know that all creation groans and is in agony even until now" (Rom 8:22). In the light of creation's joys as the garment of heaven's joy, how is our indifference to creation's enjoyments the reason for creation's groanings? How does a deep reverence for creation assure the termination of creation's groanings?

The Eve of Imperishability

WORD

"You would have suffered eternal death, had he not been born in time. Never would you have been freed from sinful flesh, had he not taken on himself the likeness of sinful flesh. You would have suffered everlasting unhappiness, had it not been for this mercy. You would never have returned to life, had he not shared your death. You would have been lost if he had not hastened to your aid. You would have perished had he not come" (St. Augustine, bishop).[48]

REFLECTION

Salvation can hardly be understood apart from God's purpose for human existence. Human life loses sight of its purpose when a meaning we give it places God on the periphery of our existence. To live life for reasons that relate it only to this world is to alienate it from the joys of the imperishability it was destined to experience. The very essence of human life makes the joys of imperishability imperative! This is the purpose that defines the sanctity of human life. To live for lesser reasons is to run the risk of becoming their likeness, perishability.

December 24 is the eve of Christ's nativity, when first was announced the glad tidings that the Savior of humankind's imperishability had come to relink humankind to its roots. On this eve, St. Augustine cries out, "Awake, mankind! For your sake God has become man."[49] To what are we to awaken? The message of this eve proclaims that the birth of Jesus enabled humankind to be back in touch with the sanctity of its existence. When Jesus took our flesh, humanity was restored to its truest nature. The birth of Christ restated once and for all that humanity belongs to God, and it is that belonging that grants sanctity to human life.

Jesus Christ embraced human belonging to confirm that humanity's primary belonging to God's creative intent made human life worth the joy of its divine becoming. The sacredness of human life does not arise from a so-called sanctity of human choice alleging human freedom to be the ultimate judge of life's earthly tenure. When human choice is proclaimed sovereign, egomania sires perishability.

Jesus was born into a wasteland existence where human choice's right to dispose of life ruled sovereignly. Jesus came into this desert of perishability so that human life's restoration to imperishability might become the fulfillment of its ancient longing. Because Jesus Christ chose to appear in the wasteland of humankind's alleged sovereignty to indict its shallowness, the creativeness of God once again was freed to cry out, "Let there be light" (Gen 1:3).

Bathed in this light, it has been the joy of all men and women to see light where only darkness reigned. They rejoice: we need not suffer eternal death; we are freed from sinful flesh; we are not condemned to everlasting futility; we are reowned for eternal life; we are re-created to enjoy the imperishability of God's image and likeness.

It is Advent's role to announce again and again salvation's joyful news. On this eve of the remembrance of Christ's first coming, the whole world echoes Isaiah's glad tidings:

> How beautiful upon the mountains
>   are the feet of him who brings glad tidings,
> Announcing peace, bearing good news,
>   announcing salvation and saying to Zion,
>   "Your God is King!". . .
> Break out together in song,
>   O ruins of Jerusalem!
> For the LORD comforts his people,
>   he redeems Jerusalem.
> The LORD has bared his holy arm
>   in the sight of all the nations;
> All the ends of the earth will behold
>   the salvation of our God (Isa 52:7-10).

We began our Advent reflections with the question "If God does not seem near to you, who moved?" Advent's voice is firm: "God hasn't!" Advent's voice is the voice of John the Baptist, who asked only that we "make straight in the wasteland a highway for our God" (Isa 40:3). On this highway of repentance, God, who never moved, longs to rush toward our lostness that we might be found and reowned. God is Immanuel, and our wasteland of perishability is where God longs to find us, be with us, and raise us to the joys of imperishability.

"Come, come," Advent beckons on this eve of Christ's nativity. Tomorrow, his natal day, Jesus beckons, "Come follow me."

QUESTIONS FOR YOUR REFLECTION

1. Why do you exist? What is the only imperishable that will accompany you as you depart from this earth?

2. Why is it futile to understand salvation apart from God's purpose for human existence?

3. What purpose of human life is the rationale behind abortion, consumerism, and euthanasia? Why do their advocates attribute "sanctity" to human choice? Is human choice, of itself, sacred?

4. What, for you, is Advent's most consoling message?

DECEMBER 25, THE BIRTH OF CHRIST

"Christian, Remember Your Dignity!"

WORD

"Christian, remember your dignity, and now that you share in God's own nature, do not return by sin to your former base condition. Bear in mind who is your head and of whose body you are a member. Do not forget that you have been rescued from the power of darkness and brought into the light of God's kingdom" (St. Leo the Great, pope).[50]

REFLECTION

St. Leo offers us three reasons for remembering human dignity. We were created to "share in God's own nature," we are members of the body of Christ, and we have been empowered to dwell in "the light of God's kingdom." The saintly Pontiff was not playing with metaphors when he invited people to remember the dignity of human life. Pope

Leo insists that we were created to be, in union with Christ, the incarnation of God's nature, Christ's body, and heaven's radiant light. No other creature shares that dignity.

Our likeness to God's nature does not make us clones of God. To the contrary, our sharing in God's life enriches our humanity to magnify the presence of Christ in the world. We remember human dignity when we pursue our vocation to grow humanly so that Christ may more fully be born at the center of humanity. A spirituality that keeps God "up there" or "out there" runs the risk of letting our humanity make room for lesser gods at the center of an existence in which *we* are cloning their image and likeness.

St. Leo offers us a second reason for remembering our human dignity. "Bear in mind who is your head and of whose body you are a member." Christ's presence continues to exist here upon earth in a body of which he is the head and we the members. This needs to be remembered because a persistent longing to be present with Jesus at his manger birthplace in Bethlehem may be evidence of a less-than-healthy spirituality forming our lives. St. Leo offers a much healthier foundation for spirituality: "Through the sacrament of baptism, you have become a temple of the Holy Spirit."[51] This temple is not the manger where Jesus was born, hallowed as his birthplace may be. The temple of the Holy Spirit is the body of women and men through whose transformed communion God's Holy Spirit is forming the very presence of Christ, now!

Christmas does not invite us to build a spirituality primarily on a wishful-thinking foundation of being present at Christ's birth in Bethlehem. Rather, the feast of Christ's nativity reminds us to be a Eucharistic people who gather frequently as the body of Christ to be nourished by his sacramental presence. We gather at the Eucharist not to enkindle longings for the past presence of Christ in the manger at Bethlehem but to recall the past as it reminds us of the continuing substance of Christ's incarnation both now and in the future.

The Eucharistic words "This is my body" (Matt 26:26) challenge us to look beyond both Bethlehem's historical and Eucharist's sacramental appearances to that body of men and women whose human presence re-presents the body of Christ. Sacraments have little significance for us when we fail to embrace their meaning in our daily lives. The Eucharist pleads with us to remember not only the dignity of Christ's human body in Bethlehem and his sacramental Body on the altar but also to remember the indescribable dignity of all human beings who embody Christ's presence in the world around us. This is the presence the Eucharist calls us to touch as we "take this [bread] and eat it" (Matt 26:26).

Finally, St. Leo asks us to remember our dignity because the birth of Jesus brought us "into the light of God's kingdom." While our imaginations can be quite vivid, they reel before the astonishing news that Christ's birth has given all of us the capacity to possess the light of heaven within us. It is at this point that imagination gives way to the faith that bears us "up on eagle wings" (Exod 19:4) and brings us into the presence of God's light, whose radiance continues to grace this world. The light of faith is as brilliant today as it was around the hill country near Bethlehem long ago.

The kingdom of God is not a light reserved for life after death. Jesus announced that "the reign of God is already within your midst" (Luke 17:21). The headship of Christ with his body here upon earth is not mere metaphor. The glorified presence of Christ seated at his Father's right hand in heaven is also the presence that gives his body headship here upon earth. The light of heaven, present in Christ's headship, is the same light that fills all of us. We experience it not as we experience earthly light but as the light that God's gift of faith provides. Faith is the way we touch the presence of Jesus, who claimed "I am the light of the world" (John 8:12). This is the touch of light that transforms us and enables us to become the likeness of God.

The nature of God, the body of Christ, and the light of Christ—these are the reasons St. Leo asks us to remember our dignity as we celebrate the Feast of Christ's Nativity. We possess a dignity worth remembering not just once a year on December 25 but every day of the year. What obligates us to celebrate the Eucharist is the nobility of our human dignity graced with the presence of Christ. Indeed, *noblesse oblige!*

Today we pray:

> God of love, Father of all,
> the darkness that covered the earth
> has given way to the bright dawn of your Word
> made flesh.
> Make us a people of light.
> Make us faithful to your Word,
> that we may bring your life to a waiting world.
> Grant this through Christ our Lord.[52]

QUESTIONS FOR YOUR REFLECTION

1. Why is a spirituality that prefers to keep God "up there" a risk to Christ's ongoing incarnation? What does the "God up there" attitude say about our response to God's longing for our transformation into Christ's life? What is the meaning of Isaiah's name for God, "Immanuel"?

2. Along these same lines, what is the wishful thinking, I wish I could have been in Bethlehem when Christ was born, saying about one's view of Christ's *now* presence in our midst? Does this thinking reveal a conviction that leads people to think that Christ was more present in Bethlehem than he is in the least of his brothers and sisters today?

3. Can you recall anyone who was a "light" to you? Did that light give birth to a dimension of Jesus you had not experienced before?

4. Have you heard it said, "I wish every day could be Christmas"? Isn't that a possible dream, when our dignity and the dignity of all others is recognized?

Notes

1. "Justice in the World," (Washington: Publications Office of the U.S. Catholic Conference, 1971) 34.

2. St. Charles Borromeo, "A Pastoral Letter," *Acts of the Church at Milan.* See *Liturgy of the Hours* (New York: Catholic Book Publishing Company, 1976) 1:153.

3. St. Bernard, "On the Advent of the Lord," *Opera Omnia.* See *Liturgy of the Hours* 1:169.

4. St. Ephrem, deacon, "Commentary on the Diatesseron," *Sources Chretiennes.* See *Liturgy of the Hours* 1:176–177.

5. St. Anselm, "The Proslogion," *Opera Omnia.* See *Liturgy of the Hours* 1:184.

6. *Ibid.*

7. *Ibid.* 185.

8. *Ibid.*

9. St. Cyprian, "On the Value of Patience," *Corpus Scriptorum Ecclesiasticorum Latinorum.* See *Liturgy of the Hours* 1:192.

10. Eusebius of Caesarea, "Commentary on Isaiah," *Patrologia Graeca.*See *Liturgy of the Hours* 1:202.

11. St. John of the Cross, "Treatise on the Ascent of Mount Carmel," bk. 2, ch. 22. See *Liturgy of the Hours* 1:213.

12. The Dogmatic Constitution on the Church, no. 48. See *Liturgy of the Hours* 1:220.

13. Pope Paul VI, "Building the Church with Christ," *Seven Addresses on the Church* (Washington: Publications Office of the U.S. Catholic Conference, 1966) 20.

14. St. Augustine, "A Discourse on the Psalms," *Corpus Christianorum Series Latina.* See *Liturgy of the Hours* 1:227.

15. *Ibid.* 228.

16. St. Peter Chrysologus, "Sermon 147," *Patrologia Latina.* See *Liturgy of the Hours* 1:236–37.

17. St. Irenaeus, "Against Heresies," *Sources Chretiennes.* See *Liturgy of the Hours* 1:244.

18. *Ibid.*

19. Blessed Isaac Stella, "A Sermon," *Patrologia Latina.* See *Liturgy of the Hours* 1:252.

20. *The Documents of Vatican II, The Church Today,* Walter M. Abbott, ed. (New York: The America Press, 1966) no. 68.

21. *Ibid.* no. 64.

22. Pope Paul VI, "On Evangelization in the Modern World," no. 18 (Washington: National Conference of Catholic Bishops, 1976) 16.

23. *Ibid.* no. 19.

24. *Ibid.* no. 21.

25. *Ibid.* no. 41.

26. William of St. Thierry, "On the Contemplation of God," *Sources Chretiennes.* See *Liturgy of the Hours* 1:271.

27. Anthony de Mello, *Song of the Bird* (Chicago: Loyola University Press, 1983) 120.

28. *The Imitation of Christ,* lib. 2, chs. 2–3. See *Liturgy of the Hours* 1:280.

29. "The Challenge of Peace: God's Promise and Our Response," no. 2 (Washington: National Conference of Catholic Bishops, 1983), 1–2.

30. St. Irenaeus, "Against Heresies," *Sources Chretiennes.* See *Liturgy of the Hours* 1:287.

31. The Dogmatic Constitution on Divine Revelation. See *Liturgy of the Hours* 1:295.

32. St. Augustine, "Discourse on the Psalms," *Corpus Christianorum Latina.* See *Liturgy of the Hours* 1:303.

33. *Ibid.*

34. St. Augustine, "The Confessions," *Corpus Scriptorum Ecclesiasticorum Latinorum.* See *Liturgy of the Hours* 3:291.

35. St. Leo the Great, "A Letter," *Patrologia Latina.* See *Liturgy of the Hours* 1:321.

36. "Letter to Diognetus," *Funk* 1. See *Liturgy of the Hours* 1:328.

37. John J. McIlhon, "When You Least Expected Him," *Markings.* (Chicago: The Thomas More Association, Aug. 9, 1987).

38. St. Irenaeus, "Against Heresies," *Sources Chretiennes.* See *Liturgy of the Hours* 1:328.

39. Thomas Merton, *A Vow of Conversation* (New York: Farrar, Strauss, Giroux, 1988) 206.

40. Raymond E. Brown, *A Coming Christ in Advent* (Collegeville: The Liturgical Press, 1988) 62.

41. St. Bernard, "In Praise of the Virgin Mother," *Opera Omnia.* See *Liturgy of the Hours* 1:346.

42. St. Ambrose, "A Commentary on Luke," *Corpus Christianorum Latina.* See *Liturgy of the Hours* 1:354.

43. *Ibid.*

44. *Ibid.*

45. Venerable Bede, "A Commentary on Luke," *Corpus Christianorum Series Latina.* See *Liturgy of the Hours* 1:362.

46. St. Hippolytus, "A Treatise Against the Heresy of Noetus," *Patrologia Graeca.* See *Liturgy of the Hours* 1:370.

47. Pope Paul VI, "On Christian Joy," (Washington: National Conference of Catholic Bishops, 1975) 7.

48. St. Augustine, "Sermon 185," *Patrologia Latina.* See *Liturgy of the Hours* 1:379.

49. *Ibid.*

50. St. Leo the Great, "Sermon on the Nativity of the Lord," *Patrologia Latina.* See *Liturgy of the Hours,* 1:405.

51. *Ibid.*

52. The Sacramentary, Opening Prayer, Christmas—Mass During the Day (1985 International Committee on English in the Liturgy) 44.